MARCO ⊕ POLO

ICELAND

LAND

Reykjavik

ICELAND

Norwegian Sea

ATLANTIC OCEAN

NORWAY

IRELAND **GREAT BRITAIN**

www.marco-polo.com

FREE!

THE TOURING APP

shows you the way...
including routes and offline maps!

GET MORE OUT OF YOUR MARCO POLO GUIDE

IT'S AS SIMPLE AS THIS

1 go.marco-polo.com/ice

2 download and discover

GO!

WORKS OFFLINE!

SYMBOLS

INSIDER TIP   Insider Tip

★   Highlight

●●●●   Best of...

☆   Scenic view

♲   Responsible travel: for ecological or fair trade aspects

(*)   Telephone numbes that are not toll-free

PRICE CATEGORIES HOTELS

Expensive   over 23,400 ISK

Moderate   14,800–23,400 ISK

Budget   under 14,800 ISK

High-season prices for two people sharing a double room, incl. breakfast

PRICE CATEGORIES RESTAURANTS

Expensive   over 3700 ISK

Moderate   2200–3700 ISK

Budget   under 2200 ISK

Prices are for a main course in the evening, drinks not included

CONTENTS

DID YOU KNOW?
Timeline → p. 14
Whaling → p. 24
Local specialities → p. 28
For bookworms & film buffs
→ p. 60
The Vikings → p. 76
Superjeeps → S. 82
Currency converter → p. 113
Budgeting → p. 115
Weather → p. 116

MAPS IN THE GUIDEBOOK
(120 A1) Page numbers and
coordinates refer to the road
atlas
(0) Site/address located off
the map
Coordinates alre also given
for places that are not
marked on the road atlas
(U A1) Coordinates for the
map of Reykjavík inside the
back cover

(🕮 A1) refers to the
removable pull-out map
(🕮 a1) refers to the inset
map on the pull-out map

INSIDE FRONT COVER:
The best Highlights

INSIDE BACK COVER:
Map of Reykjavík

The best
MARCO POLO
Insider Tips

Our top 15 Insider Tips

INSIDER TIP ▶ **Icelandic design**

At *Kirsuberjatréð* in Reykjavík you'll not only find knitted pullovers, but also off-beat creations in felt or organza. Accompany these with elegant necklaces made of bits of hosepipe and pearls (photo above) → p. 30

INSIDER TIP ▶ **Ornithology in stone**

Artworks of a very special nature: the *stone eggs* by artist Sigurður Guðmundsson in Gleðivík, lined up along the little coast road in all colours and sizes → p. 55

INSIDER TIP ▶ **Underwater experience**

Daring divers can plunge deep down between the continental plates in Þingvallavatn → p. 43

INSIDER TIP ▶ **A world of fire**

Relive the most riveting volcano eruptions on the archipelago in the 20th century at *Museum Eldheimar*. Take a look at what lies beneath the thick layers of ash → p. 46

INSIDER TIP ▶ **Quiet and cosy**

The small hotel *Aldan* in Seyðisfjörður mixes comforts with nostalgia and is a good first or last accomodation if you travel by ferry → p. 58

INSIDER TIP ▶ **One night in August**

Reykjavík on *Culture Night* is one giant event, with music, readings and firework displays. Every year, the programme swells to include new offerings, so there's always something to discover (photo right) → p. 109

INSIDER TIP ▶ **Close-up on birds**

You can study at leisure the birds which live on and around Mývatn lake in the *museum* on its banks → p. 66

INSIDER TIP ▶ **Off to the country**

The luxurious and cosy apartments of *Hotel Grímsborgir* are reminiscent of a country estate. Relax at the hotel or take a little trip to the sights in the South → p. 51

INSIDER TIP Winter sport

Iceland in winter is more than just shopping in Reykjavík – there are a number of great winter-sport venues, too. The wide expanses of the *northwest* in particular and around *Mývatn* are ideal for cross-country skiing. If you like it a little faster, hop on a Ski-Doo → **p. 103**

INSIDER TIP Space and sound

The five connected domed rooms of *Tvísöngur* sit above Seyðisfjörður as a walkable sound sculpture. Hear the difference in your own voice in each room → **p. 58**

INSIDER TIP In Gunnar's valley

The attractive *Fljótsdalur* valley was the downfall of the heroic figure of Gunnar. So in love with the landscape – from here you have a particularly beautiful view – he remained on his farm and was killed by his enemies. A plaque tells the story → **p. 50**

INSIDER TIP Steep cliffs and rich nature

Flocks of sea birds can't be wrong – take a boat from Ísafjörður to the cliffs of Hornbjarg → **p. 78**

INSIDER TIP On the subject of seals

They gaze up at you with their big round eyes. At the *Icelandic Seal Center* in Hvammstangi you can find out how and where they live → **p. 107**

INSIDER TIP Camping for all

The *Camping Card* is ideal for families or couples – and helps to make your Iceland holiday a little cheaper. The list of participating campsites gets longer every year. The card is available via the Internet → **p. 113**

INSIDER TIP Into the ice

A walk through a glacier is surely the most intensive way to experience the ice. The *ice tunnel* in Langjökull will send shivers down your spine → **p. 81**

BEST OF...

GREAT PLACES FOR FREE
Discover new places and save money

● *Down on the farm*
The ruins of the 11th-century longhouse *Stöng,* which can be visited for free, give a vivid impression of the size and layout of farms back then. Route 32 is worth a detour on the way to the highlands → p. 52

● *Reykjavík fans*
The *Reykjavík card* is the best and cheapest way to explore the entire city as well as go swimming. Simply show your card to gain free entry to all the city's swimming pools → p. 40

● *Return transfer to the airport*
If you buy the *Flybus ticket* there and back online, you'll pay considerably less than purchasing two single tickets. It's worth to plan ahead → p. 113

● *Get pally with the puffins*
To see puffins really close up, you usually have to take an organised boat trip. On the steep coast at *Látrabjarg* the comical cliff-dwellers come up close enough for you to count the rings on their bills – for free → p. 74

● *What's geothermics all about?*
At several sites in *Hveragerði,* you can sea how geothermal energy is being harnessed to heat greenhouses and outdoor beds in the gardening centre. Head to the *hot springs area* for free information about the different kinds of steam and thermal springs (photo) → p. 48

● *Romantic spot for a dip*
The little pool at *Selárdalur,* which you can visit for free, has a charm all its own. It lies on an idyllic river, and in autumn is lit up by the Northern Lights as well as candles → p. 58

●●●● Dots in guidebook refer to "Best of..." tips

● *Great knits*

The traditional Iceland pullover is an ideal piece of outdoor kit, and at *Víkurprjón* in Vík they have a huge selection of hand-knitted models with the typical pattern around the neck. Alternatively, in true Islandic spirit, you can knit your own → p. 31, 39, 72

● *Cultural heritage: sagas*

The preserved manuscripts of the Icelandic sagas are considered cultural treasures on the Iceland. They are displayed in a specially darkened room in Reykjavík's *Culture House*. Moreover, almost every region of the country has its own heroic figures whose exploits can be tracked back in time → p. 37

● *Dance on a volcano*

The Iceland of *Heimaey* is a prime example of how the consequences of nature's menacing power can be turned to man's advantage: the hot lava heats the water; the ruins and excavations are tourist attractions. The island's inhabitants are also happy about their port protected by a fortress of lava → p. 44

● *Cascading waters*

Iceland is synonymous with waterfalls; there are thousands of them, many marvelled at daily, others completely hidden from view. The finest is probably the fan-shaped *Dynjandi* (The Thundering One), in the northwest (photo) → p. 74

● *Seething earth*

In some places on Iceland the earth's crust is relatively thin, hence the bubbling, hissing and steaming going on everywhere. If there's also an element of sulphur involved, then you're in for an aromatic experience, as at *Námaskarð* near Mývatn → p. 66

● *Warm baths*

As early as the Middle Ages, people loved bathing in warm water. Since the 20th century, natural baths are a ritual in almost every town or village, whereby a cosy chat in a hot pot is an indispensable element. The oldest pot can be looked at – but not used – in *Reykholt* → p. 72

● *Lava deserts*

Iceland is a land of volcanoes which erupt regularly. Ash clouds and lava flows are the result. The beautiful lava deserts, for example *Ódáðahraun* in the highlands, have evolved over centuries → p. 83

ONLY IN

BEST OF...

● *Under one roof*
A rainy day is an ideal opportunity to do some shopping and perhaps watch a new film in the original. The shopping malls *Kringlan* in Reykjavík and *Smáralind* in Kópavogur have heaps of shops and giant cinemas → p. 39

● *A world of experiences*
The *"Wonders of Iceland"* exhibition at Perlan is the place to go on days when grey rain clouds engulf the landscape. You have everything from glaciers, ice caves and polar light to sea and volcanos as well as dry feet guaranteed → p. 36

● *Water from all directions*
Reykjavík not only has the large swimming pool *Laugardalur*, but plenty of others, too. Sitting in a hot pot in rain or snow is a real treat. Should the breeze around your ears turn chilly, just take a dive → p. 39

● *The magic of the glaciers*
Examination of multi-coloured glacier-water specimens combined with a fine view: both are possible at the "Library of Water" *Vatnasafn* in Stykkishólmur. It is also invites quiet contemplation – as dreamt up by artist Roni Horn → p. 75

● *Music in church*
During the summer months there are regular lunchtime concerts in the *Hallgrímskirkja* in Reykjavík. The acoustics in the church are outstanding, the pale grey interior pleasantly unfussy (photo) → p. 35

● *A stroll on the beach*
What is probably Iceland's prettiest beach lies to the west of *Vík*. The water gurgles as it washes over the black lava pebbles, and you can walk for miles. Since you are bound to have your waterproofs with you on your trip to Iceland, this is a good opportunity to try them out → p. 52

RAIN

RELAX AND CHILL OUT
Take it easy and spoil yourself

● Beauty on Board
Enjoy the crossing over Breiðafjörður to Flatey in a comfortable chair aboard the gently swaying *ferry "Baldur"*. As you pass what seems like a thousand islands, you can watch the birds and maybe even spot a whale. Just don't forget to get off the boat.. → p. 77

● Into the blue
The water will carry you at the *Blue Lagoon* – just let yourself drift off, with a suitable drink to hand. If that's not relaxing enough, treat yourself to a massage, visit the sauna or slap on a mud face pack (photo) → p. 41

● A menu with a view
What an appetizer: Reykjavík and the surrounding countryside gravitate past as you gaze out from the best window seats in the revolving restaurant *Út í Bláinn* in the dome of *Perlan*. The food, too, is excellent, so a visit to this most unusual eatery is worthwhile whichever way you look at it → p. 38

● Sunset at the lighthouse
From the car park of the bird sanctuary at the *Grótta Lighthouse,* the view of the horizon sweeps across the sea and sky. Sit down for a moment and let your thoughts wander as the sun sets over the sea – the epitome of relaxation → p. 42

● Northern Lights
If you take a room at the hotel *Rangá,* you can relax in one of the hot pots outside and savour the view of the Hekla and the river Rangá. On the same spot in autumn or winter, you could be treated to the spectacle of the Northern Lights → p. 50

● Camping in the woods
A campsite bang in the middle of the forest! In *Hallormstaður* in Atlavík you can pitch your tent under the trees. Sitting out front, you will hear the leaves rustling in the treetops as you look out over the lake. Or just close your eyes and listen to the wind → p. 58

DISCOVER ICELAND!

Iceland is full of contradictions, surprises and secrets. Its archaic volcanic landscape transports you back to the primeval times of the earth's origins. In some places, the earth's crust is dangerously thin, and the bubbling, steaming holes give you a glimpse of our planet's fiery interior. What people in the Middle Ages held to be simply threatening and strange – the work of the Devil and the gateway to Hell – is used by 21st-century Icelanders to great advantage. The lava serves as building material; *geothermal energy* is transformed into electricity and the hot water heats houses and swimming pools. The Icelanders have learnt how to "dance on a volcano". The country's true wealth is its natural resources which are fundamental to the existence of the 333,000 people who live here. Alongside the *power generated from the waters* of countless glacial rivers and from the geothermal energy of this volcanic Iceland, it is above all the *fishing grounds* within the hard-fought 200-mile zone which constitute the island's economic base and which are consequently fished very carefully.

Photo: Turf houses

An almost archaic typical photo motif for Iceland: sheep in high grass before a fog-covered landscape

First and foremost, it is the varied face of the countryside which draws tourists in their thousands every year. In the south, you'll find expansive meadows with broad, black beaches washed by crashing white surf; close by, the black snouts of giant *glaciers* seem to run out of steam just before reaching the sea. In the east, the steep basalt plateaux surge upwards, into which deep fjords and narrow mountain gorges have cut a path. Wide valleys and the country's longest fjord, the Eyjafjörður, dominate the north.

Black beaches and giant glaciers

The northwest, scored by numerous fjords to form its characteristic jagged coastline, is only sparsely populated. Landslides, which at the very least block a few roads, are common during the harsh winters. The higher ground is a broad lava field scattered with boulders, an

874
Ingólfur Arnarson settles permanently in Iceland

930
Founding of the annual national assembly, the Althing, in Þingvellir and declaration of a free and independent Icelandic state

1000
Adoption of Christianity

1262
The Norwegian king is recognised as monarch

1380
Iceland and **Norway fall to** Denmark

1550
The last Catholic bishop Jón Arnason is beheaded; Den-

inhospitable moonscape of isolated peaks and mountain ranges. Add to this the hundreds of *waterfalls*: hidden, thundering, mighty and beautiful – some of them with a tale to tell, others so small you might be the first to stumble across them. All this is concentrated on a single Iceland whose closest neighbours are Greenland (300 km/185 miles to the northwest) and the Faroe Islands (500 km/310 miles to the southeast).

The Icelanders love their island and its breathtaking landscape which has formed them just as much as their origins and history. To this day, they still consider themselves the descendants of the Vikings who came here from Norway to live in freedom, away from the then king. First attempts at settlement failed; the Norwegian Flóki thought the terrain too forbidding and icy, prompting him to

> **The sagas are a national cultural treasure**

give it the name Ísland (Iceland). He came ashore in the northwest in 865 AD and stayed just one winter. Only ten years later, however, the island was permanently settled. The next 300 years, today referred to by Icelanders as the "golden age", saw a blossoming of culture on the island. Most of the events during the period of settlement were recorded in the *sagas*, Iceland's national cultural treasures. Many Icelanders are proud to point out that they are able to read the medieval texts in the original.

Dark times set in after 1262. At first, Iceland was under Norwegian rule and then fell to the Danish crown. Free trade was limited; self-determination on a national level or in legal matters was a thing of the past; a host of natural disasters laid waste to the land and killed man and beast alike. *Famines*, epidemics and extreme poverty, as described by Iceland's literature Nobel laureate Halldór Laxness in his novel Iceland's Bell, were the result. Cultural life came to a standstill. For a long time, this era cast a shadow over relations between the Icelanders and the Danes, whom they experienced as colonial masters. However, after a struggle lasting almost 100 years, independence was achieved – finally – in 1944.

While the other European countries suffered during World War II and its aftermath, Iceland profited from it in many ways. The *American occupation* occupation in par-

mark confiscates church property

1602–1854
Danish trade monopoly leads to the economic impoverishment of Iceland

1874
The new constitution grants the Althing legislative power and control of all financial affairs

1904
Hannes Hafsteinn succeeds the Danish governor as the first Icelandic Prime Minister

1944
Declaration of the Republic of Iceland in Þingvellir

ticular enabled a rapid of infrastructure on the island in the 1940s. The Ring Road and the international airport were built, and Reykjavík grew, since workers were needed to carry out these projects. In addition, a shift had taken place over the previous decades from agriculture to *fishing* which also boosted the wealth of towns and villages. The relationship between Americans and Icelanders was strained when Keflavík was designated as a base for American troops in 1946. Fear of a return to colonial rule was great, yet at the same time the Americans opened

Iceland profited from World War II

the door for Iceland to the modern era through music, cars and an attitude towards life to match. Some believe that the Icelanders were virtually catapulted from the Middle Ages into the modern age as a result.

Iceland is a modern country, and some past visitors may have been a little disappointed to find that its people no longer live in little turf houses, but in high-rise blocks built to withstand earthquakes. These days, *architects* often use Icelandic materials, as can be seen especially at the Blue Lagoon; the service building and the hotel with its famous lake are clad in lava bricks and set amidst a landscape of lava.

For many years, Iceland was considered to be a veritable paradise thanks to its steadily growing economy. The year 2008, however, showed that this prosperity was merely on loan, so to speak. After years of full employment, unemployment reared its ugly head again, and inflation reached double figures for a time. In 2011, it looked like the country was back on track and the ever-popular tunnel projects were poised to get under way once more. Aside from the fishing industry, Iceland clung on to the – not uncontroversial – practice of *aluminium production*, and tourism is as important an economic factor as ever.

Iceland welcomes visitors all year round. In summer, three months of daylight are the attraction, during which hardly anyone seems to sleep, and many work outside until midnight. In this time, the flora truly bursts into life, and even on the wide highland plateaux cushions of brilliant pink moss campion carpet the ground. The *midnight sun*, low in the sky, transforms the landscape into an enchanted golden realm and paints the glacier-topped mountains in glowing deep red and violet hues.

1952–75
"Cod wars": Iceland extends its fishing limits to 200 miles

1993 / 2001
Entry into the European Economic Area (EEA) and the Schengen Agreement

2008
A financial and banking crisis brings the country to the brink of bankruptcy

2016
Iceland's football team advances to the quarter finals of the European Championships, creating quite a sensation

2017
Early parliamentary elections saw the cabinet under the new leadership of Katrín Jakobsdóttir

What a spectacular show! Green Northern Lights shimmer through the night sky above Skaftafell

In September and early October, *autumnal colours* dominate, and the hillsides and plains resemble many-coloured patchwork blankets. During the long winter nights, you can marvel at the fascinating spectacle of the dancing, vibrating *Northern Lights* – magical, mystical and bewitching.

Dancing Northern Lights – magical, mythical and bewitching

Iceland is by no means only a land of silence – in many places, you are distinctly aware of hearing nothing but the sound of nature: the rush of the waves over pebble beaches; the thundering waterfalls; the chorus of birdsong. The first great Icelandic composer of the 20th century, Jón Leifs, was inspired by these *nature sounds*, leading him to compose such impressive works as Geysir and Hekla. Art, too, is much influenced by Iceland's natural landscape and history, as Reykjavík's museums clearly demonstrate. The young and dynamic *cultural scene* has made a name for itself on an international level, and the country has brought forth many multi-talented artists. Some are successful not only as authors, but also as painters; another is one of the founders of the band Sugarcubes and today writes children's opera. Ultimately, though, it is nature which overwhelms you in a way which has captivated so many travellers in the past and which makes you want to come back again and again.

WHAT'S HOT

1 Restaurant goes clubbing

All change A cup of coffee in the daytime followed by DJ beats in the evening *(photo)*. All age groups love *Kaffi Sólon (Bankastræti 7a | Reykjavík)*. The sound of daytime chat gives way to cocktails and loud music in the evenings. Other locations which blend day into night, *b5 (Bankastræti 5 | Reykjavík)* and the cosy *Prikid (Bankastræti 12 | Reykjavík)*, appeal to the same clientele.

All about fish

Off-beat This everyday ingredient is transformed into something very special in Reykjavík. The fishing nation can't do without this staple, but a little variety on the plate is called for. At the *Fish Market (Aðalstræti 12) (photo)*, everything revolves around the scaly sea dweller: how about teriyaki trout or monkfish with goat's cheese and coriander? The *Þrír Frakkar hjá Úlfari (Baldursgata 14)* also devotes its attention to this typical product of Icelandic kitchens, from traditional dishes such as Hákarl to grilled fish plate. The *VOX Restaurant (Suðurlandsbraut 2)* abides by its principles, but its New Nordic Cuisine gives a new take on fish.

3 Creative gear

Import-Export Not all the cool clothing is imported. The garments sold at *Kron (Laugavegur 63B | www.kronkron.com)* are colourful, unique and made of the finest materials. Youthful Icelandic knit designs are the hallmark of the label *Farmers Market*. It's definitely worth browsing through the flagship store *(Hólmaslóð 2 | Reykjavík)* in Reykjavík's trendy fishpacking district.

Vatnavinir project

Turn it on The Blue Lagoon, just outside the capital, is a household name, but there are other hot springs worth visiting scattered across the country. The not-for-profit organisation *Vatnavinir (www.vatnavinir.is)* is committed to making springs accessible so that they can be used sustainably. Among the organisation's "customers" is the country's oldest hot spring; at a family hotel in Heydalur, the water bubbles out of the ground *(www.farmholidays.is/FarmDetails /190/heydalur) (photo)*. In Krossnes, *Vatnavinir* promotes hot pots with a sea view. In the village of Drangsnes, you can hop out of your car into the hot water – where you're likely to find the odd local resident waiting for you *(on the road through Drangsnes | www.drangsnes.is)*.

4

Size isn't everything

Beer Micro-breweries are mushrooming up all over Iceland. One of the first was *Bruggsmiðjan*, which has progressed from a miniature undertaking to a most successful operation. The dark "Kaldi Dökkur" comes highly recommended. Fascinating guided tours and tastings are also on offer at the brewery in Árskógssandur *(Öldugatu 22)*. Not too far away, in Akureyri *(Furuvellir)*, the brewery *Einstök* crafts all kinds of beers from ale to double bock. The town's bars have the beer with a viking's head on the label on tap. One of the country's best beers is produced on a tiny farm. The *Ölvisholt* brewery *(photo)* doesn't have guided tours, but its chocolaty Lava Imperial Stout and Co. are available nationwide from *Vinbudin (www. vinbudin.is)*.

5

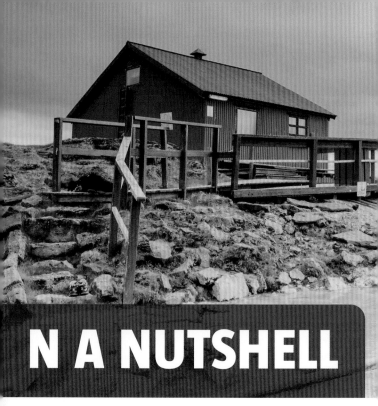

N A NUTSHELL

AMERICA

Why is Iceland's international airport named after Leifur Eiríksson? Because in fact he discovered America long before Columbus, after his legendary father Erik the Red had discovered and conquered Greenland in 982. From there, Leifur sailed west hoping to discover new land in 1000 AD. He put ashore at three different locations in what is today Canada and named them Helluland, Markland and Vínland. Some years later, other Icelanders tried to settle in Vínland but because of conflicts with the Indians returned to Iceland three years later. However, the route by ship to the New World continued to be used for collecting timber. These journeys were documented in the Icelandic sagas which were later presumably read by Columbus.

HOT POTS

The hot pot is one of the country's major attractions, whether in a natural bath tub into which warm natural source water flows or a purpose-built pot in a swimming pool or summer house. Every decent house has its own hot pot and the same applied back in medieval times. Politician and poet Snorri Sturluson (1179–1241) was an early fan of consultations in his bathtub "Snorralaug" in Reykholt which he had specially built for this purpose. Discussions and meetings are more fruitful in a relaxed atmosphere which is why, even today, communal bathing in these relaxing hot pots brings

Power up and wind down: the Icelanders have lived with all manifestations of volcanic activity since time immemorial

together politicians and managers, poets and singers; this is the place to exchange news and views. Just like most outdoor activities in Iceland, you can enjoy communal outdoor bathing all year round, irrespective of wind and weather. Is there anything better than sitting in a hot tub enjoying a drink while it is snowing around you? Just for the record: Snorri was murdered on his way between his Snorralaug and his house in 1241. Conclusion: it's safer to stay in the hot pot!

HOTSPOT FOR CREATIVITY

Iceland rates not only as a land of literature with a passion for reading; it has long since become an exciting place for music, creative arts and designers. Everybody knows who Björk and Sigur Rós are today and every year music agents travel to the "Icelandic Airwaves" festival to hear the latest Islandic sounds.

One of the latest musicians to rise to fame is the TV personality, actress and former Miss Iceland, Steinunn Jónsdóttir with her album "Steingervingur". Islandic artists do not restrict themselves to one genre only, for example Hallgrímur Helgason is both author and painter. Iceland's artists are often politically active, a fact underlined when the author and comedian Jón Gnarr became Major of Reykjavík (2010–14). Iceland's fashion designers like to use typical native materials for their creations. The purpose of the Icelandic Design Centre is not only to raise the awareness and appreciation of Icelandic design in the country but also to export it and promote collaboration with industry.

ELVES

The Icelandic elves are not figures out the pages of fairy-tales and fantasy novels, but rather the "hidden folk". Although they often reveal themselves, not many people can see them. If Icelanders are asked if they believe in the hidden people, only a few will say they do, but hardly anyone doubts their existence. Sometimes certain rocks and boulders are left alone in order to avoid upsetting the hidden elves who might be living there. Is it all true? We might never know...

GREEN POWER

Iceland is considered a global leader in terms of renewable energy. All of the island's electricity is generated from hydropower and geothermal power. No surprise really when you consider the abundant supply of both on the island. Geothermal energy is used in the form of superheated steam or hot water. Almost 90 per cent of households are heated in this way, as are over 200,000 m^2/0.07 square miles of greenhouse space, fish breeding stations, swimming pools and roads. Take a look at the island's overall electricity consumption, however, and the picture is very different: Icelanders have the highest per capita electricity consumption in the world with over 50,000 kWh per person. Private households are not to blame though. The country's industry is the major sinner, in particular the aluminium-smelting plants, which virtually eradicate the is-

When winter comes, Icelandic horses grow thick coats

land's role model status. Thousands of nautical miles are covered to import the world's main source of aluminium, bauxite, which is smelted here. Vast areas of highland have disappeared under water, for example with the Kárahnjúkkar dam in the northeast. From an environmental perspective, it makes far more sense to use the existing energy to continue using greenhouses. Since the financial crisis in 2008, there has been a drive on Iceland to produce more regionally grown vegetables. Outside greenhouses, you can see cautious attempts at cultivating arable crops and, of course, potatoes.

CUTE INHABITANTS

The island is home to the cute Icelandic ponies with their cuddly fur. Although you are surely tempted to stroke them, it's worth knowing that their owners do not appreciate you doing so. In older days, the horse was the only means of transport on the island and today they are used for tourism purposes and for rounding up sheep. Did you know that there are more "Isis" - as the Icelandic pony is popularly known - living abroad than in their native Iceland? The herds of wandering sheep are a mainstay of the island's economy. In summer you can spot them wandering across the countryside, even in the most faraway corners. There are around 450,000 sheep inhabiting Iceland and both their meat and wool are used. Where there are sheep, there are dogs and they will always give visitors an enthusiastic welcome on driving up to a farmhouse because they love visitors. The Icelandic dog is a breed of dog similar to the Welsh corgi, a friendly, long-haired breed full of energy, a classic herding dog. The arctic fox is the only land mammal which was native to Iceland before human settlement and is now commonly found in the northwest; the rest were brought to the

island by man. However, Iceland is a paradise for birds. Tens of thousands of seabirds nest on the steep rocky cliffs: black guillemot, razorbill, fulmar, gannet, guillemot and puffin. Inland there are huge colonies of pink-footed goose, and rare species of European duck, such as the harlequin and long-tailed varieties, splash about on Lake Myvatn. Often you can see the large bluish-black raven who are said to keep the God Odin informed about what the people are doing.

EVERYTHING THAT SWIMS...

...is good enough to eat. Or that's what the Icelanders believed for hundreds of years. Today, their diet is restricted to fish and shellfish but the export of seafood still plays an important role for the island's economy. Annual quotas are laid down to preserve stocks of the most important species fished – cod, haddock, redfish, saithe and capelin. High-tech processing plants operate with flexible production systems so they can react quickly to market demands. The main export regions are the USA, Japan and Europe.

For centuries, sea mammals were hunted for their meat and although the hunting of minke whales is still permitted today, most Icelanders are now conscious of the senselessness of this activity. Minke whales and orcas (killer whales) can be spotted on whale-watching excursions, as can porpoises. On the coasts, you will often come across various species of seal which also breed here.

COLOURFUL FLORA

can be found in even the most remote, inhabitable settings – you can find a diverse variety of plants and flowers in highland areas. Most species are tiny but are intensively bright in colour. Colourful meadows full of a variety of herbaceous plants, such as the purple cranesbill, thrive on the mountain slopes. On the barren plains you'll find varieties of saxifrage, for example, the pink moss campion, and along river banks the glowing purple blossoms of the arctic fireweed and carpets of green moss. Berries, fungi and brown-grey-green lichen *fjallagras* also enrich the Icelandic menu. In early summer, Iceland transforms into the "blue island" when the widely spread Nootka lupine blossoms. Once introduced to combat erosion and help with reforestation, these flowers have colonized vegetated areas and overtaken the natural flora. That said, the country's reforestation programme has been a major success and the island is no longer a barren outcrop.

GEYSERS

The Great Geysir in Haukadalur was mentioned as early as 1294, and Bishop Brynjólfur Sveinsson described it for the first time using the word "geysir", thus establishing the designation for all such hot-water spouts. Chemist Robert Bunsen studied the workings of this phenomenon on a trip to Iceland in 1846. He discovered that the water temperature increased, the further down in the geyser column he took his measurements. His explanation was that as the water depth increases, pressure rises and with it the boiling point. The pressure of the steam generated underground must consequently build up to such an extent that it is stronger than the pressure of the water above it in the 5 m/16.5 ft-deep column. The steam then forces the water upwards, causing the familiar jet of water to erupt.

FATHER'S SONS AND DAUGHTERS

Names in Iceland are a conundrum for foreigners. Most are difficult to pronounce but luckily you only need to learn the first name as people address each other by the first name only in Iceland. The second name is the father's name with the suffix *-son* (son) or *-dóttir* (daughter). The names in a typical family could look something like this: father Einar Johannson and mother Svava Eliasdottir have a son, Gisli Einarsson, and a daughter, Jorunn Einarsdottir. As you can see, there is no common family name, only patronyms, or individual father's names.

SUCCESS FOR A TINY NATION

Icelanders and football share a passionate history. A sport which was once only

WHALING

The whaling quota in Iceland was set to 239 minke whales and 154 fin whales in 2015. However, in recent years, Icelandic fishermen have not exhausted this quota because of the shrinking market for whale meat. As Japan has been one of the main consumers of whale meat, the reactor meltdown in Fukushima as a result of the tsunami in 2011 has contributed to a steep decline in demand. The international whale protection agency, WDC, maintains that this quota is still three-times higher than what the whale population can sustain. In particular, the hunting of the endangered fin whale has received much criticism, which is why Iceland did away with the hunting of this species in 2016.

Players of the national football team with – to the rest of Europe – colourful names

practised in the summer months is now possible (since 2002) all year round on indoor pitches. And the Icelandic team caught the attention of the world when they beat England in the European Championship. They rose like the phoenix from the ashes in the 2016 European Championships only to die like the phoenix in the ashes at the World Championships in 2018. Some of the Icelandic footballers are on duty all-year round because they play professional football for foreign clubs.

VOLCANIC ACTIVITY

With its 15–20 million years, Iceland is one of the youngest regions of the world from a geological point of view – and is still evolving. Volcanic activity, seething thermal zones, the movement of the glaciers and the constant drifting apart of two major continental plates are changing Iceland's landscape all the time. The active volcanic belt traverses the country from Reykjanes in the south-west to Öxarfjörður in the northeast. Two

further such areas are on the Snæfellsnes peninsula and in the south.

For geologists, Iceland is like an illustrated textbook, featuring many types of volcano and rock formations – such as ropy lava or obsidian – thermal areas, solfataras (sulphur vents) and geysers. Most of the 30 or more volcanic systems in these areas have a central volcano or a mountain range with a caldera (a large, round crevasse such as at Askja). Since the settlement of the island, around 250 eruptions, some of them lasting months or years, have taken place in 15 volcanic systems. Some 45,000 m³/1588,875 ft³ of rock has been created in the process. The most active central volcanoes are Hekla, Katla and Grímsvötn, each one clocking up over 20 eruptions. In 2010, the eruption of the volcano Eyjafjallajökull brought European air traffic to a standstill for several weeks. From August 2014 to February 2015, Bárðarbunga spewed up to 30 m³ (39 yd³) of lava into the air. In Iceland's "Hell's kitchen", things are constantly on the boil.

FOOD & DRINK

Traditionally, Icelandic cooking is simple and down-to-earth: fish, meat, potatoes, cereals and milk products. Various techniques have been used to preserve fish and meat, including souring, smoking, drying, curing or pickling in whey.

Some old recipes have lived on into the present day and are eaten particularly at the winter's end feast *þorrablót*. For the Icelanders this is a way of *driving out the winter*. Eating foods preserved in the traditional manner harks back to earlier centuries and symbolises the return of fresh foods to the table.

Only when *greenhouses* were constructed did local production of tomatoes, cucumbers, peppers, lettuce and mushrooms begin. Until then, only rhubarb and cabbage had been grown. Some supermarkets have an impressive stock of fresh vegetables and fruit, imported from all over the world. In recent years, the Icelanders have enriched their diet – largely consisting of meat and fish – by the addition of "greens" which were previously frowned upon. This variety is also reflected in the range of places to eat – from Asian restaurants through fast-food chains to rustic Viking pubs, you'll find just about everything.

When the economic crisis hit in 2008, the trend towards *regional cooking* also hit Iceland. The import of food was extremely expensive at the time as a result of the collapse of currency so the cultivation of vegetables in Icelandic greenhouses expanded. Even native cereals

Fish, fish and more fish: from dried fish to wild salmon – Iceland's chefs are dab hands with the sea's harvest

are being cultivated, a fact made possible due to climatic change and the creation of resistant types of grain. For the consumer, this is definitely an advantage. Holidaymakers should make a point of looking for typical restaurants and foods in the different regions.

Where both fish and meat are concerned, quality is a top priority, and all products are *home-produced*-. Almost everything from the rivers and the sea lands on a plate in some form or other. Apart from the usual sources of meat, foal is also on

the menu, and, in the poultry department, *svartfugl* (razorbill), whose large, colourful eggs also appear on the shelves in spring. Some supermarkets have fresh meat and fish counters, otherwise prepacked products are to be found on refrigerated shelves. There are a number of small fishmonger's shops in Reykjavík which sell auk and their eggs when in season. In some places, you can buy freshly caught fish from the fishermen as they come in to harbour. Young cooks are reviving old recipes or experimenting

LOCAL SPECIALITIES

blóðmór – Blblóðmór – Sheep's blood sausage, boiled and eaten with *lifrarpylsa*

brennivín – Icelandic aquavit nick-named the "black death" because of its label (and knock-out quality!)

hákarl – Greenland shark, fermented in open wooden crates and then dried over several months. When washed down with a slug of *brennivín*, palatable even for non-Icelanders

hangikjöt – Smoked lamb. Cooked with potatoes, béchamel sauce and peas, it is a traditional Christmas dish. Sliced and eaten cold on rye pancakes *(flat-kökur)* (photo left)

harðfiskur – Dried fish. Haddock, cod or catfish dried in the open air and served as a snack with butter (photo right)

lifrarpylsa – Liver sausage made from lamb's liver. Together with *blóðmór*, one of the family of sheep's sausages known as *slátur*

mýsa – Whey which has separated from skyr. A refreshing drink

plokkfiskur – Stew consisting of pota-toes, fish and onions

rúgbrauð – Dark, sweet bread, in some places baked in the hot springs

saltkjöt – Salted lamb, boiled and eaten cold

skyr – Cream cheese made from skimmed milk. Popular dessert with milk or cream and brown sugar

svið – Singed sheep's head. The cleaned heads are boiled in saltwater and served with mashed potatoes or swede. Eaten cold as a starter or as a packed lunch for on the road

sviðasulta – Brawn made of sheep's head in aspic

vatn – Water, direct from the spring or the tap – always enjoyable

ýmis súrmatur – Various soured meats, such as blood sausage, liver sausage and boiled ram's testicles which have been marinated in *mýsa* (whey) for 3–4 months

with them, for example, horsemeat is sometimes used instead of lamb for smoked *hangikjöt*.

Icelanders love eating – and in great quantities; individual meals are corre-spondingly lavish. A decent **breakfast buffet** includes cornflakes with *súrmjólk* (soured milk) and brown sugar, bread, a selection of cold meats, jam – made, for example, from home-grown berries –

tomatoes, cucumber and of course *síld* (herring), marinated in a variety of sauces.

Lunchtime is usually from noon to 1pm, and most of the working population are out to lunch at this time. Restaurants put on appropriate menus, consisting of soup and a fish dish for a reasonable price of around 15 euros. Among the more popular choices are *ýsa* (haddock), *þorskur* (cod) and *karfi* (redfish), either steamed or grilled.

In the afternoon, you'll find a *range of cakes*, catering to both sweet and savoury tastes. The impressive-looking creamy gateaux are loaded with calories, whereas the *pönnukökur* (crêpes), filled with cream or jam, and *kleinur* (doughnuts) are a little lighter. *Flatbrauð* is a pancake made out of rye flour and is topped with a thin slice of *hangikjöt* (smoked lamb). Sandwiches with *rækja* (shrimps) and mayonnaise are also popular afternoon snacks.

Evening meals are mostly eaten at home and are the most important of the day. At the weekend, many Icelanders like to round off the week with a visit to a restaurant. A number of the internationally trained chefs create highly imaginative dishes from local produce, often inspired by Asian or Mediterranean cuisine. The *salmon* is excellent, whether smoked or grilled. Farmed salmon is available all year round, and in summer the wild variety is fished from the salmon rivers for which Iceland is famous. *Reyktur silungur* INSIDER TIP (smoked trout) is a speciality of the region around Mývatn and tastes particularly tangy as it is smoked over juniper wood. Should you choose *lamb* as your main course, you'll have to pay considerably more than for fish (around 30 euros), but it's worth it. The *lambs* roam freely across the meadows in summer, eating only

grasses and herbs, which is why their meat has a slightly "seasoned" flavour. Another speciality is *hreindýr* (reindeer) – for venison experts a real treat. You'll often come across restaurants advertising *hvalur* (whale meat). This is fried like a steak and, as befits an animal of this size, has a pretty overwhelming taste.

Beer has now replaced the traditional mead

Due to its relatively low price, *whale meat* was once a typical staple of poor fishing families.

A sumptuous evening meal should be accompanied by wine; tap water is served with all meals. It is of such high quality that it is even exported. This is also the reason why Icelandic beer tastes so good. The trademark beverage, however, is *coffee*. It is the essential conclusion to every meal and a permanent feature of every get-together. In the evening, Icelanders like to pep it up with cognac or a liqueur. Coffee is relatively cheap, especially when you consider that the second cup usually comes free.

SHOPPING

So you might not be able to take the volcanoes with you, but maybe a candlestick or salt cellar made of lava. You hardly notice a Lava pearl necklace because it is so lightweight. The area of design in particular has plenty on offer – sometimes kitschy, sometimes creative, but always typically Icelandic. You'll find the appropriate outlets in the shopping malls *Kringlan (Reykjavík)* and *Smáralind (Kópavogur);* otherwise it's worth a foray into streets such as Laugavegur in Reykjavík city centre.

COSMETICS

A cosmetics range going under the label *Blue Lagoon* has been manufactured, based on the special minerals present in the lagoon of the same name. Apart from at the spa itself, the products are also available in tourist areas as well as in the cosmetics departments of the shopping malls. At the *Nature Baths* at Mývatn *(see p. 66)* they also sell their own skin care range, also based on minerals, which so far is only available here.

FASHION DESIGN

Since Icelanders have long been very fashion-conscious, you can buy all big-name labels here. Icelandic designer brands, however, are something special. A handbag or wallet made of fish skin is a real eye-catcher, especially if it comes from INSIDER TIP *Atson (atson.is)*. If you want to see how the fish skin is processed, then head to the tannery at Sauðárkrókur *(see p. 68)*. If you like things a touch more extravagant, head for *Spaksmannsspjarir* for fashions inspired by the Icelandic landscape *(www.spaksmannsspjarir.is)*. Unusual items made from surprising materials are to be had at INSIDER TIP *Kirsuberjatréð* in Reykjavík's Vesturgata: fish-skin bags, jewellery made from bits of plastic hosepipe or felt and organza evening dresses *(www.kirs.is)*. The Icelandic label *66° North* manufactures excellent outdoor fleece garments.

JEWELLERY

Icelandic gold- and silversmiths produce small and very fine individual pieces, some inspired by the Viking era, others incorporating the island's semi-precious gemstones and each with its own particular style. The prize-winning jewellery designed by *Dýrfinna Torfadóttir* is highly unconventional. You can buy it at a num-

Wool, fashion and cosmetics: Icelandic designers give typical native materials an off-beat twist

ber of places, including at *Epal Design* in Reykjavík, *Hotel Saga* in Ísafjörður and at the airport shop in Keflavík.

LAMB & SALMON

If Icelandic cooking is to your taste, you might like to try out some recipes at home using original Icelandic lamb. Delicious vacuum-packed lamb chops are easy to transport. You can find them in every supermarket, as well as at cooperatives such as in Hvammstangi in the North. Round off your menu with a few slices of salmon. By the way, at the *Icemarket* at the airport, you'll find a large selection of Icelandic foods.

SOUND & VISION

A beautiful coffee-table book by an Icelandic photographer is an ideal souvenir. But let's not forget music, either; you'll find a fine and up-to-date selection of CDs and help on hand to guide you

through it in Reykjavík at *12 Tónar (Skólavörðustigur 15)*.

WOOL

The classic souvenir from Iceland is of course the Iceland pullover. Wool from Icelandic sheep has superb properties: the long top layer of wool is water-repellent and the finer fibres underneath are as soft and light as mohair. On offer are a range of items, from clothing to cosy blankets.

● Beautiful, hand-knitted, models – what else? – can be found at *Víkurprjón* in Vík í Mýrdal *(Austurvegur 20 | tel. 4871250)*. Woollen items featuring classic designs are not to be found at *Gaga (www.gaga.is)*, as the designer has named herself. Some of her creations are quite crazy and unusual. The in-label for woolwear is *Farmers Market* in Reykjavík *(farmersmarket.is)*. The stools lined with sheep fur are also extremely fluffy.

31

REYKJAVÍK

MAP INSIDE THE BACK COVER
(127 D5) *(ŵ E9)*
Reykjavík is a modern and dynamic city yet retains the idyllic charm of a village. You'll get the best view over the city (pop. 125,000) and the surroundings from the tower of the Hallgrímskirkja or from Perlan.

Reykjavik is not only the economic and political heart of the country, but also its cultural capital. In 2011, Unesco named Reykjavik a "City of Literature", the fifth to bear the title. Founded just 250 years ago, this relatively young city is bursting with life and exciting places to discover. Reykjavík invites visitors to explore its diversity, ranging from design, art, culture, partying and entertainment to its sunsets and northern lights, hot dogs and gourmet menus to its small alleyways and expansive parks. Just 30 to 40 km/19 to 25 miles away are the most thrilling natural wonders in the midst of the lava landscape.

SIGHTSEEING

AÐALSTRÆTI (U B3) *(ŵ b3)*

Visiting Reykjavík's oldest street is like stepping back in time. Starting at its southern end, the foundations of a Viking longhouse from the 10th century can be viewed at *871+/-2 The Settlement Exhibition (daily 8am–6pm | admission 1650 ISK, free admission for children; also valid for Aðalstræti 10 | borgarsogusafn. is/en/thesettlementexhibition).* The artefacts on display are part of a captivating multimedia exhibition on the settlement

The tiny metropolis in the North: sights and high-tech architecture embedded in stunning countryside

CITY **WHERE TO START?**
The tourist centre is the old part of the city between the Tjörnin lake and the harbour. Central bus station: Lækjartorg. City Hall, with an underground car park, is located here, as is **Austurvöllur (U B3)** *(⤢ b3)* square with the Parliament building, Hotel Borg, Dómkirkja and cafés. From here, head for the Harbour House and the shopping street, Laugavegur.

of Reykjavík. The square opposite holds a statue of Skúli Magnússon and it's hard to believe that this was once the location for the city's cemetery. Skúli Magnússon (1711–1794) founded Iceland's first wool factory in Aðalstræti no. 10 thus laying the foundation for Reykjavík's prominence as a trading centre. This building, or what remains of it, is still standing. There are two exhibitions focusing on Iceland's history *(daily 10am–5pm, see above)*. At the end of the street stands an 18th-century warehouse from which a tun-

A tourist magnet with shops, bistros, and berths for fishing vessels and excursion boats: the old harbour

nel once led to the harbour. It was largely used to smuggle the gyr falcons, kept in the warehouse, to the ships waiting in the harbour to take them to their aristocratic European buyers.

ÁRBÆJARSAFN (0) (*m 0*)

Open-air museum featuring 27 traditional buildings, dating back to the period from 1820 to 1907. Special programmes for children are offered at weekends and you can take part in courses to learn about old agricultural methods. *June–Aug daily 10am–5pm, Sept–May 1pm-5pm, daily guided tours at 1pm (in English) | admission: 1650 ISK, free admission for children | Kistuhylur 4 | borgarsogusafn.is/en/arbaer-open-air-museum*

ÁSMUNDUR SVEINSSON SCULPTURE MUSEUM (U F4) (*m f4*)

Ásmundur Sveinsson (1893–1982) was one of the country's foremost sculptors. Many of his works are to be seen in Rey-

kjavík, in particular here at the Asmundarsafn. The studio was built in 1942 to his own plans. *May–Sept daily 10am–5pm, Oct–April daily 1pm–5pm | admission 1500 ISK | Sigtún | www.artmuseum.is*

AURORA BOREALIS (U A2) (*m a2*)

This museum explains the phenomenon of the Northern Lights, complete with photo footage – an ideal stop if you have not yet seen this natural wonder in real life. The shop sells INSIDER TIP t-Shirts in the colours of the Northern Lights. *Daily 9am–9pm | admission 1600 ISK | Grandagarður 2 | www.aurorareykjavik.is*

AUSTURVÖLLUR (U B3) (*m b3*)

In the centre of this busy square, scene of all political rallies, is the *statue of Iceland's national hero Jón Sigurðsson*, crafted by Einar Jónsson. He looks towards a grey basalt building: the seat of the Icelandic Parliament, the *Alþingishús*. It was built in 1881 and an extension was added in 2001. To the left of this stands Reykjavík's oldest church, *Dómkirkja,* from 1776. The eastern side of the square is dominated by the venerable *Hótel Borg,* founded in 1930. In summer the square is simply a favourite spot for having fun.

CITY HALL (U B3) (*ⅅ b3*)

A real architectural eye-catcher, built in 1992 on land specially reclaimed from the Tjörnin. Form and location initially earned much criticism from the population; the building detracted from the pretty row of villas which lined the shore of the inner-city lake. Today, City Hall is a popular venue for receptions and exhibitions. It is also home of the tourist information centre. The large 3D representation of Iceland is a must-see, too.

EINAR JÓNSSON MUSEUM (U C4) (*ⅅ c4*)

The sculptor and painter Einar Jónsson (1874–1954) is not an entirely uncontroversial figure in Iceland, famous for his intense symbolist works of hero-cult style sculptures. However, almost every influential Icelander was cast in bronze by Jónsson. The sculpture garden behind the museum is also well worth a visit. *Tue–Sun 10am–5pm | admission 1000 ISK | Eiríksgata 3 | www.lej.is. Garden open all year round, free admission*

HAFNARHÚS (HARBOUR HOUSE) ★ (U B3) (*ⅅ b3*)

The former warehouse on the harbour is the setting for some fantastic exhibition rooms. Focal point of the collection is the work of Icelandic artist Erro, famous for his large-scale paintings which borrow heavily from the comic genre. Born Guðmundur Guðmundsson, this visual artist created around 400 works of art and most of them are on display here. The cafeteria offers views over the harbour. *Daily 10am–*

5pm (Thu until 10pm) | admission 1650 ISK | Tryggvagata | www.artmuseum.is

HALLGRÍMSKIRKJA ★ (U C4) (*ⅅ c4*)

You can spot the 76 m/250 ft-high tower of this church from far away; it was named after the pastor and author of the Passion Hymns Hallgrímur Pétursson (1614–74) and is now a famous city landmark. Built to a highly unconventional design by Guðjón Samúelsson, the church can accommodate 1200 worshippers. Pétursson took his inspiration from the vertical arrangement of basalt columns when designing the sweeping tower façade. Construction took over 40 years, and the church was finally consecrated in 1986; the huge organ was added in 1992. Regular ● *organ concerts* are staged during the summer months – a real acoustic treat in these bright, generously proportioned surroundings. A *statue of Leifur Eiríksson,* the man who "discovered" the New World, stands in front of the church. *Tower: May–Sept daily 9am–9pm, Oct–April daily 9am–5pm | elevator trip up the tower 900 ISK / hallgrimskirkja.is, regular concerts held in summer*

HARPA ★ (U C2–3) (𝄞 c2–3)

Approaching Reykjavík from the sea, you can't fail to notice the multi-storey, multi-coloured building on the harbour. The Harpa Concert Hall and Conference Centre has a fascinating glass façade by artist Olafur Elíasson. In addition to event venues, the building houses a number of shops and bars as well as the Icelandic pavilion from the World's Fair in 2010 that shows a 15-minute film about the island on a 360° screen. *Austurbakki 2 | harpa.is, guided tour 1500 ISK – dates on the website, toilets 300 ISK (in summer)*

LISTASAFN ÍSLANDS (NATIONAL GALLERY) (U B3–4) (𝄞 b3–4)

Collection of Icelandic art covering the 19th century to the present day and shown in changing exhibitions. Attractive café. *Summer daily 10am–5pm, winter Tue–Sun 10am–5pm | admission 2000 ISK | Fríkirkjuvegur 7 | www.listasafn.is*

OLD HARBOUR (U A–B 1–2) (𝄞 a–b 1–2)

Once the flourishing hub of the fishing and marine industry, most of the shipping companies have now left and the buildings have been transformed into designer boutiques, restaurants, cafes, galleries and museums. The trendy new district stretches from the Örfirisey peninsula in the west to the docking points for smaller cruise ships close to Harpa. The best way to explore the area is by bike or even Segway. The city's best café

– *Haiti* – is housed in the former green workshops. Reykjavík's best ice cream is served at *Valdís* where you can try an Icelandic speciality, liquorice ice-cream. Once a herring factory and warehouse, the Marshall House is now home to a cutting-edge museum for contemporary art, *Nýlistasafn (Tue–Sun noon–6pm, Thu noon–9pm | free admission | www. nylo.is).* The avant-garde *Kling & Bang gallery* is also based here as well as the studio of the internationally acclaimed Icelandic artist Ólafur Elíasson.

Grandagarður Street leads you to the peninsula of Örfiresey. Do not let the large warehouses distort your impression – behind the façade, you'll find small enterprises with factory outlets such as the chocolate maker, *Omnom,* which uses extremely high-quality cocoa beans roasted with nuts to produce their sumptuous chocolate. They also offer guided tours through the production premises. The packaging is just as good as its content with a wolf's face adorning every bar.

PERLAN ★ (U D6) (𝄞 d6)

Perlan ("the pearl") is the futuristic landmark of Reykjavík. This mirrored glass dome, in which the sun, clouds and the sky are all reflected, is built on top of six huge hot water tanks. The tanks stored up to 20 million litres of geothermal water from the region of Reykjavík to heat flats, swimming pools and pavements. Today, only two of the tanks are still in operation while the others house the ● *Wonders of Iceland* exhibit which takes you inside a chilly artificial glacier cave and offers an exploration of the glaciers. Augmented reality depictions of the Northern Lights and Icelandic landscape are on display in the other tanks. This sensational exhibition is ideal for families *(daily 8am–7pm | admission*

2900 ISK, 2 adults +2 children 5800 ISK | www.perlanmuseum.is/en). There is a 360-degree viewing deck around the mirrored dome where you can enjoy the panoramic view to the Snæfellsjökull Glacier. There are also wraparound views from the bistro-style restaurant *Út í Bláinn* ("Into the Blue") inside the dome *(daily 11.30am–9pm | tel. 420 27 27 | utiblainn.is | Expensive).* There is a regular shuttle bus operating between Perlan and the city centre.

PHALLUS.IS (U E4) (∅ e4)
Penises from all species of mammal – and since 2011 even from a human being – are on display here. The museum also has a number of penis curiosities and artistic works from around the world. *June–Aug daily 9am–6pm, Sept–May-daily 10am–6pm | admission 1700 ISK | Laugavegur 116 | www.phallus.is*

TJÖRNIN (U B3/4) (∅ b3/4)
The northern banks of the city lake, Tjörnin (locally called the Pond) is a hive of activity and popular with locals and children. This lake at the heart of the city echoes with the honks and squawks of more than 40 species of visiting birds including ducks, geese, swans and different types of seagulls. Farmhouses once lined the southern banks but today the lake is surrounded by car parking spaces and walks around the lake. In summer, the lake is a hotspot for locals who come to picnic and enjoy lunch outdoors. Why not join them? **INSIDER TIP** Grab a delicious salad, take a seat on the grass and enjoy a relaxing lunch in true Icelandic style!

VÍKIN – MARITIME MUSEUM
(SJÓMINJASAFN) (U B2) (∅ b2)
Old ships and other artifacts tell the story of the fisheries over the ages. Regularly

The 76 m/250 ft-high Hallgrímskirkja with the monument to Leifur Eiríksson

changing exhibitions round out this museum's programme. The coast guard vessel Óðinn, built in 1959, once served in the Cod Wars, but now it is docked at the entrance. It also has a shop and a restaurant with a patio on the water. *Daily 10am–5pm | guided tour of the ship 11am, 1pm, 2pm, 3pm | admission 1500 ISK, Óðinn 1300 ISK, joint ticket 2600 ISK | Grandagarður 8 | borgarsogusafn.is/en/reykjavik-maritime-museum*

ÞJÓÐMENNINGARHÚS
(CULTURE HOUSE) ● (U C3) (∅ c3)
Venue for changing exhibitions on various aspects of Icelandic culture and history. The collection of medieval manuscripts – recordings of the Eddas and Sagas – is particularly impressive and is Iceland's most important cultural treasure. *May–15 Sept daily 10am–5pm, 16*

Sept–April Tue–Sun 10am–5pm | admission 2000 ISK | Hverfisgata 15 | www.culturehouse.is

HLEMMU MATHÖLL (U D4) (*m d4*)

This former bus terminal is now a popular food court with ten different restau-

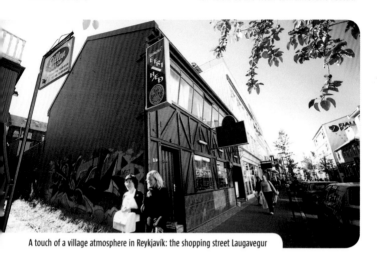

A touch of a village atmosphere in Reykjavík: the shopping street Laugavegur

ÞJÓÐMINJASAFN (ICELANDIC NATIONAL MUSEUM) (U B4) (*m b4*)

Excellent overview of the culture and history of the country from the first settlers to Icelandic society today. All sorts of temporary exhibitions. The well done multimedia presentations as well as the minimalist architecture have earned the museum a prize. Shop and café. *May–15 Sept daily 10am–5pm, 16 Sept–April Tue–Sun 10am–5pm | admission 2000 ISK | Suðurgata 41 | www.thjodminjasafn.is*

FOOD & DRINK

CAFÉ HAÏTI ⊗ (U B2) (*m b2*)

Enjoy fantastic coffee in a small bistro at the old harbour. Different fair-trade coffees are on offer, plus small homemade sweet treats as well as soups and sandwiches. *Mon–Fri 6am–9pm, Sat/Sun 7am–9pm | Geirsgata 7b/Fisherman's Wharf 2 | tel. 5 88 84 84 | Budget*

rants, bistros and cafes to choose from. It's a great place to kick off your evening and serves multicultural foods varying from Asian to vegetarian. If you're self-catering, INSIDER TIP you can buy good bread and Icelandic vegetables here *Daily 8am–11pm | Laugavegur 107 | hlemmurmatholl.is | Budget–Moderate*

INSIDER TIP KAFFIVAGNINN (U B2) (*m b2*)

Savour the good quality fish dishes overlooking the harbour. This is where the fishermen come to eat, too (and have done so since 1935). *Mon–Fri 7am–9pm, Sat/Sun 7am–9.30pm | Grandagarður 10 | tel. 5 515 9 32 | Budget*

ÚT Í BLÁINN RESTAURANT ● ⋰ (U D6) (*m d6*)

This bistro-style restaurant inside the mirrored dome of Perlan offers the ultimate view over Reykjavík. It focuses on fresh seasonal and local ingredients where Icelandic culinary traditions meet sophisticated European cuisine to create new tastes. *Daily 11.30am–11.30pm | on Öskjulið, Varmahlíð 1, Perlan | tel. 420 27 27 | utiblainn.is | Expensive*

SHOPPING

The main shopping streets in Reykjavík are *Laugavegur, Hverfisgata* and *Skólavörðurstigur.* Don't miss the *Eymundsson* bookshop or the CD stores *Skifan* and INSIDER TIP *12tónar.* Here, you'll find the hottest sounds Iceland's music business has to offer.

There are a range of Icelandic and international outlets as well as cafés and cinemas in the ● *Kringlan* and *Smáralind* shopping malls in Kópavogur. At the *Kolaportið flea market* on the harbour, you're bound to discover stuff you never knew you needed *(Sat/Sun 11am–5pm)!*

OMNOM CHOCOLATE FACTORY (U B1) (*bb b1*)
The chocolate bar with the wolf on the front, aka Iceland's best chocolate, is made here. You can also take a tour of their production premises. *Mon—Thu 11am—6pm, Fri 11am—noon, 1pm-6pm, Sat noon—4pm | guided tours Mon—Fri 2pm, 3000 ISK (in English), children between 7 and 15: 1500 ISK | Hólmaslóð 4 | www.omnomchocolate.com*

THE HANDKNITTING ASSOCIATION OF ICELAND ● (U C3) (*bb c3*)
A wide range of handmade hats, socks, sweaters and blankets from traditional to fashionable are sold at this knitting collective. You can also buy Icelandic yarn, needles and knitting patterns and do it yourself. *Mon–Fri 9am–6pm, Sat/Sun noon–6pm | Skólavörðustígur 10 | tel. 552 18 90 | www.handknit.is*

SPORTS & ACTIVITIES

BIKE & SEGWAY
You can explore the city on your own with *Reykjavík Bike Tours,* which also hire out electric bikes. Or you can join a guided tour by Segway (1 person costs 37,000 ISK, the more participants there are, the cheaper it is). *Ægisgarður 7, at the Old Harbour, tel. 897 27 90 (by Segway), tel. 694 8956 (by bike), daily in summer from 10am, in winter Fri/Sat from 10am.* The route along the coast as far as the bird sanctuary at the Grótta Lighthouse is ideal for an excursion by bike. Bike hire is also available at *Borgarhjól (Hverfisgata 50* (U C3) (*bb c3*) *| tel. 5 51 56 53).*

DIVING
PADI Dive Center offers diving excursions around Reykjavík, on the Reykjanes peninsula and in Þingvallavatn. Night dives as well as snorkelling are also available. Snorkelling or diving excursions in the Silfra Rift available from 14,900 ISK. *Hólmaslóð | tel. 578 62 00 | www.dive.is*

WELLNESS ●
If you just want to relax, head for *Vesturbæjarlaug (Hofsvallagata* (U A3) (*bb a3*) *| admission 900 ISK):* this is where the city's rich and famous meet up. Bathe among locals away from the tourist hub at the *Grafarvógslaug bath (Dalhús | Grafarvógur).* Right next door to the large Laugardal spa in Reykjavík is the spa resort *Laugar (www.laugarspa.com)* with its wide range of wellness treatments.

BEACH

NAUTHÓLSVÍK (0) (*bb 0*)
Yes, Reykjavik does have its own beach on the edge of the Öskjuhlíð recreational area. Thanks to the hot spring, you can enjoy a water temperature of 20 degrees.

In summer, it is heaving with sunbathers since the entire beach is just 100 m/328 ft long – but it's a special resort nonetheless. *15 May–15 Aug daily 10am–7pm, 16 Aug–14 May Mon–Fri 11am–2pm, Mon, Wed 5pm–8pm, Sat 11am–4pm, winter 600 ISK | Nauthólsvegur | nautholsvik.is*

ENTERTAINMENT

KAFFIBARINN (U C3) (*m c3*)
This disco and bar is a must-visit for anyone who has read Hallgrimur Helgason's "101 Reykjavík". *Bergstaðastræti 1*

LOW BUDGET

INSIDER TIP SLIPPBARINN (U B2) (*m b2*)
A favourite spot among the locals with music on Wednesdays as well as other events. A great place to hang-out and enjoy breakfast, brunch or dinner. *Myrargata 2 | tel. 5 60 80 80 | www.slippbarinn.is*

AUSTUR (U B3) (*m b3*)
A trendy club. Your evening's entertainment can kick off here. *Thu 8pm–1am, Fri/Sat 8pm–4.30am | Austurstræti 7 | Facebook, keyword Austurclub*

WHERE TO STAY

BORG (U B3) (*m b3*)
Jóhann frá Borg named his hotel Borg ("castle") after himself and had it built using the prize money he won in America as a successful wrestler. Situated directly on the Austurvöllur, the hotel is still a luxury establishment, decorated with memorabilia from Jóhann as well as its wild era during the 1950s when it housed a dancehall. *56 rooms | Pósthússtræti 11 | tel. 51 14 40 | www.hotelborg.is | Expensive*

HÓTEL CABIN (U E3) (*m e3*)
One of the more reasonably priced hotels. The rooms are a little on the small side, but have all the essentials, from minibar to shower. The hotel also has **INSIDER TIP** rooms without daylight (don't forget, it doesn't get dark in summer!). *65 rooms | Borgartún 32 | tel. 5 11 60 30 | www.hotelcabin.is | Moderate*

LOFT HOSTEL ☺ (U C3) (*m c3*)
Certified eco-hostel. Rooms from a dorm with 8 beds to an en suite double (6 rooms). *94 beds | Bankastræti 7 | tel. 5 53 81 40 | www.lofthostel.is | Budget–Moderate*

Famous bathtubs: the Blue Lagoon is a popular place to relax, especially in winter

INFORMATION

TOURIST INFORMATION CENTRE (U B3) (⚏ b3)
Aðalstræti 2 | tel. 5 90 15 50 | www.visit reykjavik.is

WHERE TO GO

BESSASTAÐIR (127 D5) (⚏ D–E9)
The residence of Iceland's president lies on the Álftanes headland and is visible from Reykjavík. The windows of the *church*, which was built between 1780 and 1823, feature motifs from Icelandic history. Near the altar, memorial plaques hang in memory of past presidents. *Irregular opening times*

BLÁA LÓNIÐ (BLUE LAGOON) ★ ● (126 C6) (⚏ D10)
The most famous pool in Iceland lies, encircled by a landscape of lava, 40 km/25 miles to the south-west on the Reykjanes Peninsula *(45 min. by car, regular bus connections)*. The water comes from the geothermal power plant nearby, in other words wastewater. This clever marketing strategy attracts thousands of guests each year. The cloudy-blue lake gets its colour from the minerals and algae they contain, which also have proven healing properties in the treatment of skin disorders. Bathing in the warm water (38°C/100°F) full of salts and minerals is relaxing for body and mind, and a peeling with a silica mud mask is a great way to thoroughly cleanse your skin. Other spa offerings include massages and facial treatments. The spa's *restaurant (tel. 4 20 88 00 | Moderate–Expensive)* serves everything from light dishes to gourmet menus. Very crowded in the summer! *240 Grindavík | tel. 420 88 00 | www. bluelagoon.com | from 6990 ISK: tickets must be purchased online in advance, you'll receive a ticket with the date and precise time of your visit*

HAFNARFJÖRÐUR (127 D5) (⚏ E9–10)
Fancy meeting a few elves and Vikings? Then Hafnafjörður is the place for you. Situated 12 km/7.5 miles to the south of

Iceland's most important site for over 1100 years: Þingvellir – National Park and World Heritage Site

Reykjavík, its excellent harbour made it an important trading post. To this day, the harbour remains a major commercial centre, not least because of the aluminium smelting plant Straumsvík located close by the town.

Hafnarfjörður was built in the *Búrfellshraun* lava field, which defines the character of the site. It is said that huge elf colonies are hidden in the lava formations, and, following a corresponding plan, you can even take a walk through the imaginary dwellings of the fairy folk *(Tourist Information Office | tel. 5 85 55 00 | www.visithafnarfjordur.is)*. The Vikings, too, felt at home here. Every year, there is a rather over-the-top Viking Festival, organised by the owner of the restaurant *Fjörukráin (Strandgata 55 | tel. 5 65 12 13 | www.vikingvillage.is | Expensive)*.

GRÓTTA LIGHTHOUSE ● ☀
(127 D5) *(ᗰ E9)*
The Grótta Lighthouse sits at the furthermost tip of the *Seltjarnarnes* peninsula.

When the tide is out, you can easily walk to the lighthouse from the beach and climb up to the top. An official bird sanctuary is not far from the beach. Its car park is a popular destination year round because it offers a beautiful view of the sea that stretches as far as Snæfellsjökull when the skies are clear. A lovely footpath along the coast leads to this spot.

ÞRÍHNÚKAGÍGUR (127 D5) *(ᗰ E10)*
34 km/21 miles southeast along the 417, 20 minutes by car. There is a shuttle service available from Reykjavík. The trip takes you inside a volcano but don't worry, the Þríhnúkagígur has been inactive for the last 4000 years. The entrance to this unique experience starts near the Blafjöll ski resort. *Tel. 519 56 09 | admission 44,000 ISK | www.inside thevolcano.com*

VIÐEY (127 D4–5) *(ᗰ E9)*
Historically and culturally, the little island in the Kollafjörður fjord to the north of the city is a charming place for a day

trip. The first settlers were recorded here as early as the 10th century, but the oldest surviving building was constructed in 1753–55. It is the oldest stone building in the country, today a restaurant (*Budget*). The tiny church next door dates back to the year 1774. The signposted footpaths on the island lead you eastwards to the ruins of a village which boasted an international port until the beginning of the 20th century. The west of the island is the setting for Richard Serra's ensemble of standing stones, Afangar, which harmonises perfectly with the landscape and Reykjavík in the background. *Ferry from Sundahöfn, Skarfa-bakki | daily 10.15am–5.15pm every hour; from Viðey 10.30pm–6.30pm | 1500 ISK*

ÞINGVELLIR ★ (121 E4) (*F9*)

In terms of the Icelanders' sense of national identity, Þingvellir ("Parliament Plains") is the most important place in the country. It was included in the list of Unesco World Heritage Sites in 2004. This is where all historically significant events in Icelandic history have taken place: from the declaration of the free state in 930 down to the founding of the Republic of Iceland in 1944. The site, 35 km/22 miles to the east of Reykjavík, was chosen to host the original Althing for its size, reachability for most settlers and the presence of water and grazing areas for their horses.

From the observation point, with adjoining *information centre (daily 9am–6pm | toilets 200 ISK, parking 500 ISK | www.thingvellir.is)*, you have a fine view across the landscape, including Iceland's largest lake, *Þingvallavatn* (85 km^2/915 ft^2), the mountains surrounding it and the *Almannagjá* ("Everyman's Ravine"), and the track that runs through it. From the *Lögberg* ("Law Rock"), the speaker recited the laws; former execution sites are located close by. To the north of the Almannagjá is the *Öxarárfoss* waterfall, which was artificially constructed, presumably in the 10th century, to allow the waters of the Öxará to flow into the plain, to the horses.

In geological terms, too, Þingvellir is highly significant. It is the continuation of the Mid-Atlantic ridge, where the Eurasian and North-American plates are still drifting apart, as demonstrated by the two ravines, *Almannagjá* and *Hrafnagjá* ("Raven's Ravine") running from the north-east to the south-west. Measurements have shown that Þingvellir is sinking by 8 mm/0.026 ft and widening by 2 cm/0.79 inches every year.

For divers, **INSIDER TIP** the descent into the *Silfra rift* between the continental plates to a depth of almost 15 m/50 ft is a memorable experience. There are even night dives on offer *(www.diveiceland.com)*.

THE SOUTH

The countryside in the South is picture-postcard stuff, with green meadows and pastures and broad, black sandy beaches; further east, these give way to the sandar plains, formed by meltwater deposits, at the foot of the Mýrdalsjökull glacier.

Since this is one of the most active volcano zones, eruptions are frequent occurrences. Eruptions of sub-glacial volcanoes, such as the Eyjafjallajökull in 2010, are particularly dangerous. This one caused not only devastating flooding, but also threw up an ash cloud which brought worldwide air traffic almost to a standstill. Farmers in the region were badly affected, as their fields were smothered by a layer of ash. Yet only six months later, little was still to be seen of the ash itself which above all had coloured the glaciers black. Resourceful farmers sold the ash to tourists – a real big seller! In 2011, there were further eruptions destroying part of the Ring Road.

The geothermal energy in the South is used to heat the many greenhouses; you can also get an idea of its power at the famous geyser in Haukadalur or at the Hellisheiði power plant.

HEIMAEY

(128 A6) *(꒰ G12)*★ ● **The Vestmannaeyjar Islands ("Westmen Islands", about 15 in total) lie to the south-west of Iceland; the southernmost of these,**

Geysers and legends: Iceland's "market garden" lies in the flourishing landscape of this still active volcanic region

Surtsey, was only formed in 1963–67 and is now a protected area.

The largest and only inhabited island is Heimaey, whose roughly 4200 inhabitants live from fishing and fish processing. The island came to fame on 23 January 1973 when a new volcano erupted. Lava shot out of a 1.6 km/1 mile-long crevasse, gushing out, smothering the houses and threatening to close the entrance to the harbour. The eruption lasted five months, and the ash buried a third of all buildings. Today, Heimaey is a green island again, whose residents see the lava as a welcome source of building material. From Eldfell and the old ✲ Helgafell volcano you get a panoramic view of the entire island as far as the south coast of Iceland and the Eyjafjallajökull and Mýrdalsjökull glaciers.

The "Herjólfur" ferry plies between Landeyjahöfn and Heimaey several times a day, in stormy weather from Þorlákshöfn. *Return ticket: 2520 ISK (from Landeyjahöfn), 6720 ISK (from Þorlákshöfn | tel. 4 8128 00 | www.eimskip.com*

On Heimaey, signs like these mark old roads that have been buried by lava

SIGHTSEEING

INSIDER TIP ELDHEIMAR

The "fire world" museum that opened in 2014 documents the volcano eruptions on Heimaey. The creation of Surtsey can be seen in part through an excavated house that was buried under ash in 1973. You can hear first-hand how loud an eruption actually is. *May–14 Oct daily 11am–6pm, 15 Oct–5 May daily 1pm–5pm | admission 2300 ISK | Gerðisbraut 10 | eldheimar.is*

KLETTSVÍK

A whale sanctuary opened here in March 2019 and its first guests are two beluga whales. You can only visit the bay by boat.

SKANSINS

The fortifications above the harbour were constructed by the Danes in the 16th century, but they could not repel the assault by North African pirates in 1627 who carried off half the population into slavery. Parts of their ship's gear can be seen at the Folk Museum. A replica *stave church,* a present from Norway to the Icelanders in 2000 on the occasion of the 1000th anniversary of Christianisation, stands alongside the site. Also close by is *Landlyst,* Iceland's first maternity hospital (1847), now a museum. *Museum June–Aug daily 11am–5pm | admission 500 ISK*

STÓRHÖFÐI

A coastal hike along the western shores of the island to its most southerly peak Stórhöfði is an enjoyable experience. On a clear day, it also offers amazing views of the uninhabited neighbouring islands. Thousands of sea birds can be spotted nesting in the cliffs. The large colonies of puffins are particularly worth seeing. Stórhöfði also has a weather station and a splendid view over to Surtsey. A sign points to INSIDER TIP the archipelago's youngest island.

SURTSEY (128 A6) (*G12*)

An subsea volcanic eruption formed the island over a period of four years. The process began on 14 November 1963, and the lava flow finally came to a halt on 5 June 1967. Since then, surf and climatic influences have permanently changed the face of the island which is now a strictly protected area and was granted World Heritage Site status by Unesco in 2008. For tourists, boat excursions or sightseeing flights are the only opportunity to take a look at Surtsey. Information: *Viking Tours (see below)*

FOOD & DRINK

BROTHERS BREWERY

This local brewery offers guided tours with beer-tasting (three beers included in the price 2990 ISK). Its brew won a national prize in 2016. Tickets online. *Vestur-vegur 5 | thebrothersbrewery.beer/en*

GOTT
Popular among locals for its good food made with fresh ingredients, ranging from fish to vegetarian dishes. *Bárustigur 11 | tel. 4 813060 | Budget–Moderate*

SLIPPURINN EATERY
This former machinery room at the shipyards has been turned into a cosy restaurant. The menu reflects tradition, combined with fresh herbs and new flavour ideas. *Strandvegur 76 | tel. 4 811515 | Moderate–Expensive*

SPORTS & ACTIVITIES

You can book excursions by boat around the island, including bird- and whale watching trips, at *Viking Tours (Suðurger-ði 4 | tel. 4 88 48 84 | www.vikingtours.is)*. If you're looking to hike in Eyjaferðir but are less keen on going it alone, why not join a guided hiking tour (2–3 hrs). Prices and dates available on request. *Fax-astígur 33 | tel. 481 10 45 | tourist.eyjar.is*

BEACH
There is a splendid beach along the west coast to Stórhöfði which is a popular spot for (sun)bathing in summer.

WHERE TO STAY

SUNNUHÓLL
Modest rooms, also sleeping-bag accommodation. Kitchen and common room. *7 rooms | Vestmannabraut 28| tel. 4 812900 | www.hostel.is | Budget*

ÞÓRSHAMAR
Well-equipped rooms, central location, whirlpool and sauna. Staff at the hotel can also help you organise tours of the surrounding region. *24 rooms | Vestmann-nabraut 28 | tel. 4 8129 00 | www.hotel vestmannaeyjar.is | Moderate*

INFORMATION

TOURIST INFORMATION CENTRE
Located in the Folk Museum. *Ráðhúströð | tel. 4 813555 | www.vestmannaeyjar.is*

HVERAGERÐI

(127 E5) *(∅ F10)* **Its sheltered location in a valley and the thermal springs have made Hveragerði Iceland's "market garden".** Numerous greenhouses provide warmth and shelter to small vegetable plants. It is also the site of the state-run

Peppers planted, cultivated and harvested in Iceland's greenhouse capital in Hveragerði

Horticultural College and its experimental gardens and research departments. Alongside vegetable growing, tourism is a further important economic factor for the 2500 inhabitants. More and more artists have also relocated here in recent years, giving Hveragerdi a reputation as a "hippie village".

SIGHTSEEING

THE QUAKE

This exhibit in the shopping centre *Sunnumörk* shows the aftermath of the earthquake in May 2008. The exhibition includes objects which were demolished during the earthquake which reached 6.3 on the Richter scale. You can also experience how an earthquake feels in the earthquake simulator (500 (ISK). *Sunnumörk 2–4 | free admission*

THERMAL AREA ●

One of the town's many thermal areas is situated right in the centre of town. Here you can find out more about the different springs, their uses and geological structure. *June–Aug Mon–Fri 10am–6pm, Sat/Sun noon–4pm, April, May, Sept Mon–Sat 9am–5pm | free admission; guided tours possible | Hveramörk 13 | tel. 4 83 50 62*

FOOD & DRINK

RESTAURANT VARMÁ ● ⚘

"Slow Food" with a view of the river and excellent dishes made from Icelandic products, such as foals or cod. *Hverhamar | tel. 4 83 49 59 | Moderate–Expensive*

SPORTS & ACTIVITIES

You can sign up for riding excursions of various lengths organised by *Elðhestar* (*Vellir | tel. 4 80 48 00 | www.eldhestar.is*). The adventure of rounding up sheep at the end of summer is a fantastic experience for experienced riders.

SUNDLAUGIN LAUGASKARÐI

One of Iceland's oldest and prettiest pools with a stylish architecture and relaxing atmosphere. 50 m pool, hot pots, sunbed and sauna. *15 May–15 Aug Mon–Fri 6.45am–9pm, Sat/Sun 10am–7pm, 16 Aug–14 May Mon–Thu 6.45am–8.15pm, Fri 6.45am–5.15pm, Sat/Sun 10am–5.15pm | 900 ISK | Reykjamörk | tel. 483 41 13*

HEILSUSTOFNUN NLFÍ

Although its main function is a rehab centre, it also offers treatments for everyone including mud baths, massages or herbal baths. The centre also has its own baths. *Grænumörk 10 | heilsustofnun.is*

WHERE TO STAY

FROST OG FUNI

Stylish rooms, decorated with contemporary art works. Pool, sauna and hot pot on site. *14 rooms | Hverhamar | tel. 4 83 49 59 | www.frostandfire.is | Expensive*

INFORMATION

UPPLÝSINGAMIÐSTÖÐ SUÐURLANDS (SOUTH ICELAND INFORMATION)

In the shopping centre. *Sunnumörk 2–4 | tel. 4 83 46 01 | www.south.is*

WHERE TO GO

HELLISHEIÐI (127 E5) *(𝄢 F10)*

Just 18 km/11 miles to the west of Hveragerði is the *Hellisheiðarvirkjun* geothermal power plant, situated in a high-temperature zone in the Hengill Range. Steam and hot water are pumped to the surface from a depth of over 2000 m/6560 ft. The steam is used to generate electricity and the hot water to heat the glacier water. This fresh water is then fed into Reykjavík's district-heating network. Find out more about the technology, current projects and the region as a whole at the plant's visitor centre. Cafeteria. *Daily 9am–5pm | admission including*

guided tour from 1500 ISK, children up to 12 years free | tel. 591 2880 | www.geothermalexhibition.com (cheaper online)

REYKJADALUR (127 E5) *(𝄢 F10)*

Approx. 4 km/2.5 miles to the north. If you take the road leading north out of town, you'll reach the footpaths to Reykjadalur (Steam Valley). There is a car park and café next to the starting point. The walk to the hot springs takes one hour and you'll also come across INSIDER TIP Klambragilslaug, an outdoor natural hot pot where you can take a plunge into the warm river. Be prepared to share it with crowds in summer. It's important to wear sturdy shoes for walking in this area because of the extremely hot, often steaming, holes in the ground.

HVOLSVÖLLUR

(128 A5) *(𝄢 G11)* **Commercial centre for the whole region, Hvolsvöllur's 900 inhabitants work largely in the retail and service sectors.** The region's first cooperative society was founded here in the 1930s, not least because it was a favourable location for farms in the South.

SIGHTSEEING

LAVA CENTRE

This interactive museum is an amazing hands-on learning experience where you can spend the whole day. Learn everything there is to know about volcanoes, earthquakes and Iceland's birth story. You literally feel the earthquake and can hear the lava erupting. The rooftop view of the peaceful and green surroundings is relaxing. *Daily 9am–7pm | film + exhibition 3200 ISK, children 12 and upwards 1650 ISK, family ticket 5940 ISK | Austurvegur 14 | tel. 415 5200 | lavacentre.is*

SAGA CENTRE

This is a good place to get a first insight into Njál's Saga and general living conditions in the Middle Ages. Corresponding tours of the area are on offer. Iceland's most popular saga revolves around wise Njál and his friend Gunnar, who fall victim to the thirst for revenge of Gunnar's wife, Hallgerður. *Daily 4pm–10pm | admission free | Hlíðarvegur*

FOOD & DRINK

KATLA

The restaurant inside the Lava Centre mainly serves dishes incorporating regional ingredients as well as vegetarian options. A popular favourite among locals. *Daily 9am–9pm | Moderate*

WHERE TO STAY

HVOLSVÖLLUR

Cosy hotel with friendly staff. The only accommodation in the town itself. The restaurant offers excellent international cuisine. *63 rooms | Hlíðarvegur 7 | tel. 4 87 80 50 | www.hotelhvolsvollur.is | Moderate*

RANGÁ ● ⅍

Luxury with a fine view is on offer at this hotel with a country-house feel, situated 4 km/2.5 miles to the west of Hvolsvöllur. The INSIDER TIP seven suites are a big hit, but the standard rooms cater to all needs, too. *44 rooms, 7 suites | Suður-landsvegur | tel. 4 78 57 00 | www.hotel ranga.is | Expensive*

INFORMATION

TOURIST INFORMATION

At the Saga Centre. *Austurvegur 8 | tel. 4 87 80 43 | www.south.is | daily in summer*

WHERE TO GO

HEKLA ★ ⅍ (128 B4) (𝔐 H10)

The most notoriously active volcano on Iceland is the 4 km/2.5 miles-long fissure vent, Hekla, 50 km/31 miles north-east of Hvolsvöllur. The 1491 m/4655 ft-high massif is visible from a distance and was considered the gateway to Hell until well into the 18th century. The many outbursts have turned the area around Hekla into an impressive lava-clad landscape. The easiest ascent is from the north and is rewarded by a stunning view across the highlands. A four-wheel drive will take you almost to the top. The *Hekla Centre* is an excellent source of information *(daily 10am–10pm | at the Hótel Leirubakki on Rte. 26 | admission 900 ISK)*.

HLÍÐARENDI (128 B5) (𝔐 H11)

The farm and what is supposedly the burial mound of Njál's friend Gunnar lie some 15 km/9.3 miles east of Hvolsvöllur INSIDER TIP in the picturesque *Fljótsdalur* valley, with its verdant slopes and many waterfalls. Instead of fleeing for his life, Gunnar, captivated by the beauty of his farm, remained in the country and was slain. From here, you have a fabulous view of plain and river, encircled by green sloping hills. The little church completes this idyllic picture-postcard scene.

SELJALANDSFOSS (128 B5) (𝔐 H11)

20 km/12 miles east is one of Iceland's most popular waterfalls, the 40 m/131 ft high Seljalandsfoss. It belongs to a whole group of smaller waterfalls which thunder off the vertical escarpments of the Eyjafjallajökull volcano. What's special about the Seljalandsfoss waterfall is the fact you can walk behind the cascading veil of water. Make sure you take your waterproofs!

ÞÓRSMÖRK ★ (128 B–C5) *(ℳ J11)*
Some 40 km/25 miles east of Hvolsvöllur at the end of the mountain road F 249 is the Þórsmörk valley in the foothills of three protective glaciers. Numerous hiking trails criss-cross the area which is ringed off by torrential glacier rivers and is popular with day-trippers due to its lush vegetation. There is a kiosk and a campsite.

Starting in Þórsmörk, you can set off on a four-day trek to *Landmannalaugar (132 C4)* *(ℳ J10)* or hike in two days to *Skógar (132 B5)* *(ℳ J11)*. *Ferðafélags Íslands (Fí | Mörkin 6 | Reykjavík | tel. 5 68 25 33 | www.fi.is)* and *Útivist (Laugavegur 178 | Reykjavík | tel. 5 62 10 00 | www.utivist.is)* offer guided hikes and accommodation in mountain huts.

SELFOSS

(127 F5) *(ℳ F10)* **The small town of Selfoss (pop. 6500) is the main trading centre of agricultural produce in the South.**
Opened in 1929, a milk dairy is still in operation here today which makes the traditional Skyr dairy product (see p. 28). Selfoss is an ideal base for exploring the south of the island.

FOOD & DRINK

FJÖRUBORÐIÐ ⋇
Famous for its king prawns and with a sensational view out to sea! *Eyrarbraut 3a | Stokkseyri | tel. 4 83 15 50 | Moderate–Expensive*

KAFFI-KRÚS
Cosy, nostalgic, serving fine pastries and cakes. *Austurvegur 7 | tel. 4 82 12 66 | Budget*

WHERE TO STAY

GESTHÚS
These little wooden houses, including kitchen and bathroom, are great for families. *22 cabins | Engjavegur | tel. 4 82 35 85 | www.gesthus.is | Budget*

INSIDER TIP ▶ HOTEL GRIMSBORGIR
In the midst of the countryside in the south, you'll find great rooms and apartments with fireplaces and a Hot Pot. The hotel also features a prize-winning restaurant. It is easy to get to many destinations from here. *28 rooms, 10 apartments | Ásborgir 30 (on no. 36) | tel. 5 55 78 78 | www.grimsborgir.com | Expensive*

The water spurts almost 20 m/65 ft into the air out of the Strokkur geyser

SELFOSS

INFORMATION

UPPLÝSINGAMIÐSTÖÐ ÁRBORG
April–Sept | Eyravegur 2 | tel. 8 99 86 63 | tourinfo.arborg.is

WHERE TO GO

GEYSIR ★ (128 A3) *(ₘ G9)*
The thermal area 65 km/40 miles to the north-east of Selfoss is the site of the *Great Geysir*, whose 14 m/46 ft-diameter pool is surrounded by fascinating sinter deposits. Just 100 m/328 ft away, the *Strokkur* geyser regularly spouts plumes of water into the air. There are many smaller springs, from turquoise to red in colour, depending on the minerals occurring. The view from **INSIDER TIP** ❋ *Laugarfell* is particularly rewarding.

GULLFOSS ★ (128 B2) *(ₘ H9)*
One of Iceland's most stunning waterfalls lies just 7 km/4.4 miles from the Great Geysir: the Gullfoss ("golden waterfall"). The glacial river Hvítá plunges down in twin cascades, at 90 degrees to each other, into the *Hvítárgljúfur* gorge. The 31 m/102 ft-high waterfall and gorge are protected sites. There is an exhibition about Gullfoss at the upper car park, a shop and a café.

REYKHOLT (128 A3) *(ₘ G9)*
A hissing and steaming township 40 km/24 miles northeast of Selfoss. This is where most of Iceland's vegetables are grown using geothermal energy. In the huge, bright greenhouses at Friðheimar *(daily noon–4pm, recommended to reserve in advance | tel. 496 88 94 | fridheimar.is)*, staff sell the produce and offer delights made with the tomatoes they grow – like the Healthy Mary, a-watering drink made of green tomatoes and ginger. Their tomato soup is also Iceland's best.

VÍK Í MÝRDAL

(128 C6) *(ₘ J12)* Vík is the most southerly village in Iceland, whose 300 inhabitants live from trade and tourism. It is situated at the foot of the ❋ Reynisfjall ridge (340 m/1115 ft) amidst green meadows and surrounded by black sandar plains and pebble beaches.
The ● beaches at the foot of the Mýrdalsjökull rate amongst the most beautiful; some feature basalt columns or accessible caves. Birdwatchers will find thousands of seabirds. Vík lies at the heart of the 9500 km² (3668 mi²) *Katla Geopark (www.katlageopark.is)* that stretches from Hvolsvöllur up to the Vatnajökull.

SIGHTSEEING

REYNISDRANGAR
Three rocky basalt stacks that resemble a three-masted ship rise from the sea to

---

LOW BUDGET

There are a number of pretty campsites, for example directly next to the Skógafoss waterfall or in Herjólfsdalur on Heimaey.

The tomatoes and strawberries sold directly at the greenhouses are a really good deal. Just look for the roadside signs, especially in *Flúðir,* which is not far from Geysir and Selfoss.

● *Stöng* is a genuine longhouse from the 11th century which was excavated in 1939. The covered ruin – reached via Rte. 32 – can be visited at any time. *Free admission*

Vík í Mýrdal: gigantic cliffs line the coastline as far as the rock crags of Reynisdrangar

the south of Reynisfjall, the highest of them measuring 66 m/216 ft.

FOOD & DRINK

SVARTA FJARAN

The Black Beach restaurant lies directly at the Dyrhólaós estuary. Alongside tastily prepared dishes, including vegetarian options, homemade cakes are also on the menu. *Daily 11am–8pm, longer in summer | at the end of route 215 | tel. 571 27 18 | blackbeach.is | Budget*

WHERE TO STAY

WELCOME PUFFIN HOSTEL

Cosy: rooms with bath and sleeping-bag accommodation. Good restaurant. *21 rooms | Víkurbraut 26a | tel. 4 87 12 12 | www.vikhotel.is/puffinhostel | Budget– Moderate*

INFORMATION

TOURIST INFORMATION BRYDEBÚÐ

beginning of May–15 Sept | Vikurbraut 28 | tel. 4 87 13 95 | www.vik.is

WHERE TO GO

DYRHÓLAEY ☀ (128 C6) (*Ø J12*)

The promontory to the west of Vík rises 120 m/395 ft out of the sea and takes its name – door hill island" – from its archway. A lighthouse, built in 1910, stands on the cape. From here, you have a breathtaking view of the sea and glacier landscape.

SKÓGAR ★ (128 B5) (*Ø J11*)

32 km/20 miles west of Vík, an imposing waterfall, *Skógafoss,* thunders 60 m/197 ft into the valley. When the sun shines, people say you can see the shimmering chest of gold hidden behind the waterfall by Skógar's first settler. When a boy once tried to fetch the chest, he only managed to grab the handle, which is now on show at the *Skógar open air Museum (June–Aug daily 9am–6pm, Sept–May 10am–5pm | café: June–Aug daily 10am– 5pm | admission 2000 ISK | www.skoga safn.is)*. This museum describes, among other things, the history of island transport.

The stylish *Hótel Skógar (12 rooms | tel. 4 87 48 80 | www.hotelskogar.is | Expensive)* has ☀ a number of rooms with a view of the waterfall. Good restaurant.

THE EAST

The East has two distinct faces – on the one hand, the area to the south of the Vatnajökull glacier from the Skeiðarár-sandur sandar to Höfn and, on the other, the fjord landscape of the east coast, with its steep, towering basalt ridges.

These formations consist of the oldest types of rock on the island. Basalt, easily recognisable by its column-like structure, dominates, but the somewhat surreal colour spectrum of the mountains – dependent on climatic and light conditions – is down to the presence of rhyolite.

Today, the small coastal villages and towns are fighting for survival as young people in particular are flocking to the towns. The region was revitalised thanks to the aluminium smelting plant in Reyðarfjörður.

DJÚPIVOGUR

(131 E3) *(ᗈ R7)* **Old houses and a small marina characterise the face of this over 400-year-old trading post, whose 440 inhabitants still live from fishing.**

In the centre, you'll find the 200-year-old *Langabúð*, a former shop now housing a museum and café, and, next door to it, the cooperative building from the 19th century. In the summer, the area is populated by countless birds. The *Búlandsnes* promontory, peppered with lakes, is a designated birdwatching site; a number of signs have been erected with information on what you can expect to see. The *bird and minerals museum (in the summer 10am–6pm |www.birds.is)* provides more information.

Between glaciers and fjords: the fascinating world of the Vatnajökull ice cap and old, idyllic trading posts

The INSIDER TIP stone eggs by Sigurður Guðmundsson, 34 sculptures in the shape of birds' eggs around the harbour *Gleðivík*, are an attractive addition to the village. The coloured, polished natural stones resemble the real things, laid by the species native to Djúpivogur – just a lot bigger!

SIGHTSEEING

LANGABUÐ
Memorial collections of the sculptor Ríkarður Jónsson and the politician Ey-steinn Jónsson. Both men hail from the region. *June–Aug daily 10am–6pm | admission 1000 ISK*

WHERE TO STAY

FRAMTÍÐ
Sauna, solarium and large rooms. In the older part of the hotel, the rooms are more modest. The restaurant specialises in good fish dishes. *46 rooms | Vogaland 4 | tel. 4 78 88 87 | www.hotelframtid. com | Moderate–Expensive*

INFORMATION

DJÚPIVOGUR INFORMATION
*June–Aug | Bakki 3 | tel. 478 82 04 | www.
djupivogur.is*

ft). The spot is well known as a source of beautiful stones and renowned as an excavation site for zeolite crystals. Even more fascinating are the scolecites, needle-sharp crystals made of radial clusters,

Motorboats and small fishing cutters compete for space at the small harbour of Djúpivogur

WHERE TO GO

INSIDER TIP ▶ **PAPEY** ☆ (131 E3) *(∅ R8)*
Until the year 900 AD, Irish monks lived on the largest of the islands off Djúpivogur; you can still see ruins from the period and an abandoned farm. Papey is an ideal destination for birdwatching. *June–Aug | from 1pm an approx. 5-hr trip with guide: 20,000 ISK | Papeyjarferðir | tel. 4 78 81 19 | djupivogur.is/ Djupivogur/Nattura/Papey*

TEIGARHORN (131 E3) *(∅ R7)*
4 km/2.5 miles away, there is a nature reserve named after the Teigarhorn farm at the foot of the pyramid-shaped basalt mountain *Búlandstindur* (1069 m/3507

good examples of which are on display in the museum (usually 1pm–3pm).

EGILSSTAÐIR

(125 E5) *(∅ R5)* **Around 2300 people live in this relatively new town (founded in 1944), now the centre of the east region.**
The national forestry office of Iceland is based here as is a jazz club and the cultural centre *Sláturhús (slaturhusid.is)*. Egilsstaðir is a good place to start for trips into the eastern highlands, the small coastal villages as well as to the Lagarfljót lake (also known as Lögurinn) and to the Hallormsstaður forest.

SIGHTSEEING

MINJASAFN AUSTURLANDS

The *East Iceland Heritage Museum* documents life in the region from the time of settlement down to the 19th century. Two permanent exhibitions deal with life in the country and with reindeer who only live in the east of Iceland. *June–Aug daily 10am–6pm | admission 1000 ISK | Laufskógar 1 | www.minjasafn.is*

FOOD & DRINK

KAFFI NIELSEN

Located in a pretty old house, this cosy restaurant is busy all day long. The leafy outdoor terrace is popular on sunny days. The Italian-inspired dishes are made from Icelandic ingredients. *Tjarnarbraut 1 | tel. 4 71 26 26 | Budget–Moderate*

SPORTS & ACTIVITIES

BIKE HIRE

How about taking the 68 km/42 mile bike tour around the Lagarfljót Lake – in training for the annual tour in August? *3500 ISK a day. Egilsstaðastofa, Kaupvangur 17 at the camp site*

BAÐHÚSIÐ SPA

The Gistihúsið Lake Hotel has a spa area with hot pot, sauna and more importantly relaxing lake views. You can spend the whole day here, alternating between massages and snacks. *Daily 10am–10pm, bookings required for treatments | admission 3500 ISK | Egilsstöðum 1–2 | tel. 471-1114*

WHERE TO STAY

EDDA

Central location. Some of the spacious rooms are over two floors; ideal for families. *52 rooms | Tjarnarbraut 25 | tel. 4 44 48 80 | www.hoteledda.is | Budget–Moderate*

INFORMATION

EAST ICELAND INFORMATION CENTRE

Kaupvangur 17 (campsite) | tel. 4 71 30 60 | www.visitegilsstadir.is, www.east.is

WHERE TO GO

BAKKAGERÐI (125 F4) (*M S4*)

Take the 65 km/40 miles to the north and you'll discover Bakkagerði, a tiny hamlet surrounded by a mountainous landscape, framed by a backdrop of rugged and colourful rhyolite and basalt peaks. The village stands at the foot of the small Álfaborg hill ("elf town"), where the elf queen supposedly lives, a must-see for elf lovers. The place is also popular with ornithologists who come here for up-close viewing of the nesting puffins. They are in touching distance, but get too close and they will disappear

---

⭐ **Hallormsstaður**
Iceland's one and only "proper" forest is by the Lagarfljót lake
→ p. 58

⭐ **Jökulsárlón**
Cruise on a boat between shimmering blue and green icebergs
→ p. 61

⭐ **Skaftafell**
At the foot of Iceland's largest glacier, Vatnajökull, in the National Park of the same name, is a green paradise of walking trails, hot springs and glacier tongues → p. 61

MARCO POLO HIGHLIGHTS

inside their nesting caves. The best time for puffin-watching is from the start of June to mid-August.

HALLORMSSTAÐUR ⭐ (125 D6) *(⇆ Q6)*
Iceland's largest woodland and reforestation area, with a stock of trees up to 100 years old, lies 12 km/7.5 miles to the south. Take a fascinating walk through the educational forest in which a broad range of conifers and deciduous trees grow. Thanks to the favourable soil conditions and the almost continental climate, the trees enjoy ideal growing conditions. The *Hotel Hallormsstaður (35 rooms | tel. 47 24 00 | www.hotel701. is | Moderate–Expensive)* is quiet and prettily situated. In addition, there are wooden cabins and a more modest guest house. Riding excursions are also offered. The beautiful ● *Atlavík campsite* is for the romantic at heart; here, you can sleep under the trees, directly by the shore of Lagarfljót lake.

KÁRAHNJÚKAR DAM (130 C2) *(⇆ O7)*
The new, well developed road 910 leads to an information platform from where you can see the dam and the 57 km² /22 miles² *Hálslón reservoir.* Building the dam was very controversial since it has meant the destruction of a part of the Dimmugljúfur gorge. The power plant itself is situated a little to the south of Végarður (129 C2) *(⇆ Q6)*. Since its construction, Iceland's environmental movement has taken on a new dimension.

LAGARFLJÓT
(125 D–E 4–6) *(⇆ Q–R 4–6)*
3 km/1.8 miles wide and 30 km/18.6 miles long, the lake is fed by a number of glacial rivers and narrows to form the Lagarfljót river. Legend has it that a giant worm-like monster, Ormur, lives on the bed of the lake! At the Atlavík campsite, you can hire pedalos and rowing boats to explore the lake. *2500 ISK | tel. 8 47 00 63*

SEYÐISFJÖRÐUR (125 F5) *(⇆ R5)*
If you arrive by ferry, the picturesque village of 800 inhabitants, 27 km/17 miles east of Egilsstaðir, is your first point of contact with Iceland. In the 19th century, this used to be the largest commercial settlement; the well preserved wooden houses date back to this period. Alongside museums and summer concerts, Seyðisfjörður is a good starting point for hikes in the eastern fjord region. The small INSIDER**TIP** *Hótel Aldan (9 rooms | Norðurgata 2 | tel. 4 72 12 77 | Moderate)*, a mixture of comforts and nostalgia, is located in one of the historic houses.
The German artist Lukas Kühne has created a "walk-in" artwork comprised of five linked domes (2–5 m in diameter and 2–4 m high) with his space and sound sculpture INSIDER**TIP** *Tvísöngur (www.visitseydisfjordur.com/tvisongur).*

SKRIÐUKLAUSTUR (125 D6) *(⇆ Q6)*
A monastery stood here, on the southwest bank of the Lagarfljót, in the 16th

century. In 1939, author Gunnar Gunnarsson built a 1000 m²/10,764 ft² house to plans by German architect Fritz Höger. Today, it is home to a cultural centre which, among other things, stages exhibitions about Gunnarsson and also has a great café. *Tel. 4712990 | www.skriduklaustur.is*

GAMLABÚÐ

This museum of local history, the geology of the Vatnajökull, and nature lies in the old town centre at the harbour. In two other buildings, boats and other artifacts tell about the lives of the fisher-

A sky blue church before a lush green meadow: a typical image for picturesque Seyðisfjörður

HÖFN

(131 D4) *(ⓜ Q9)* **This village of 1700 inhabitants, whose name simply means "harbour", is the administrative and commercial centre for the south-east.**

Located in a picturesque setting at the foot of the Vatnajökull ice cap, Höfn – or to give it its full name Höfn í Hornafjörður – was a trading post in the 19th century. Some old buildings from the time still stand on the harbour and today house the *Folk Museum.* There is also a small shopping centre. Close to the harbour, you'll find the *recreation area* and the ⓢ INSIDER TIP *Ósland Bird Sanctuary,* home to the great northern diver, Arctic tern and whooper swan.

men in the 19th century. *June–Aug daily 9am–7pm, May/Sept daily 9am–6pm, otherwise daily 9am–5pm | admission free | Heppuvegur 1 | www.vatnajokulsth jodgardur.is*

GLACIER JEEPS

Drive over Iceland's largest glacier first by four-wheel-drive and then the last leg of the journey up the Vatnajökull by snowmobile *(e.g. 3-hour excursion with 1 hour on the skidoo per person 24,000 ISK).* Once you've arrived on the glacier, the tour operator caters for guests in the Jöklasel hut, Iceland's highest restaurant (840 m/2766 ft). *Descent from the ring road, junction F 985 | tel. 478 10 00 | www. glacierjeeps.is | available all year round*

HÖFN LOCAL GUIDE

Exploring Höfn with Hulda is fun and enjoyable because she knows so much about the place. She offers walks with yoga and you can dine with the locals. *Hafnarbraut 41 | tel. 864 49 52 | hofnlocalguide.com*

FOOD & DRINK

ÞÓRBERGSSETUR MUSEUM RESTAURANT 🌿

The excellent restaurant at Þórbergur Centre in *Hali,* 60 km/37 miles to the west, uses ingredients from its own farm.

The museum honours the life of the writer Þórbergur Þórðarson (1889–1974). Very tasty cakes! *Tel. 8 67 29 00 | www.hali.is | Moderate*

WHERE TO STAY

EDDA

Attractive location by the sea (terrace!) and next to the Ósland Bird Sanctuary. Refurbished rooms with shower/WC. *36 rooms | Ránarslóð 3 | tel. 4 44 48 50 | www.hoteledda.is | Moderate*

FOR BOOKWORMS & FILM BUFFS

The Atom Station – The novel by Nobel prize-winner, Halldór Laxness, reflects the unease in Iceland when the Icelandic Parliament decided in 1946 to allow the USA to set up a base at the Keflavík airfield (first published in 1948)

Independent People – Also by Laxness, this epic novel tells the story of life in rural Iceland of the early 20th century, a far cry from today's ultra-hip Reykjavík, but well worth reading for its black humour and sharp characterisation. (1946)

Volcano Island – Pictures of Iceland and the changed glacial landscape following the eruption of Eyjafjallajökull in 2011, captured by renowned photographer Sigurgeir Sigurjónsson.

Metalhead – a film by Ragnar Bragason. As a child, Hera experienced the death of her brother first-hand. She tries to become him, becoming a fan of heavy metal rock music and all the more radical in her actions. Iceland's rugged landscape shines in the background (2013)

Iceland Sagas – Magnus Magnusson explores the legendary tales which form Iceland's cultural heritage in their historical and geographic context. (2005)

101 Reykjavík – Film of the same-name cult novel by Hallgrimur Helgason with plenty of music, off-beat humour and crazy characters. (2000)

Iceland 63°66°N – Stefan Erdmann's three films are an invitation to immerse yourself in some beautiful images. The aerial pictures give you the impression of looking at a painting. Excellent soundtrack, also in English. (2 DVDs, 2011)

Screaming Masterpiece – The film (DVD) for lovers of Icelandic music: a 2005 documentation including loads of concert clips.

Angelica grows on the slopes surrounding the Svartifoss Waterfall in Skaftafell National Park

HÖFN

Top hotel in town, with all amenities and a decent restaurant. *68 rooms | Vikur-braut 24 | tel. 478 12 40 | hotelhofn.is | Expensive*

INFORMATION

HÖFN VISITOR CENTRE

At the museum on the harbour. *Heppuvegur 1 | tel. 470 83 30 | www.visitvatnajokull.is*

WHERE TO GO

JÖKULSÁRLÓN ⭐ (130 B5) *(ⓜ O10)*

The *Breiðamerkurjökull* glacier calves into this 200 m/656 ft-deep lake, 75 km/46 miles south-west of Höfn; the scene is one of countless blue-black icebergs drifting across the backdrop of the Vatnajökull. Enjoy some fascinating perspectives on a boat trip on the lagoon, which, in the main season, you should book ahead. Bookings: *tel. 478 2122 | www.icelagoon.is.* After your trip, you

can recharge your batteries at the *restaurant (June–Aug | tel. 478 2122 | Budget)* with its fine view across the lagoon.

SKAFTAFELL ⭐ (130 A5) *(ⓜ N10)*

Right in the middle of the Vatnajökull National Park – at 13,600 km^2/5250 miles^2, the largest in Europe – is the green idyll of Skaftafell, 135 km/84 miles west of Höfn, which extends between the icy tongues of the Morsárjökull and Skaftafellsjökull glaciers. Over 210 species of plant grow in the region; bird life, too, is plentiful and varied. There are many hiking trails criss-crossing the park. Popular spots with visitors are the *Svartifoss* waterfall and ⋇ the *Sjónarsker* observation point, facing out over the glacier and the desert-like plain, the Skeiðarársandur. You can also take part in a guided hike up Iceland's highest mountain, *Hvannadalshnúkur* (2119 m/6952 ft). Information at the *Service Centre (tel. 478 300 | www.vip.is)* in the park.

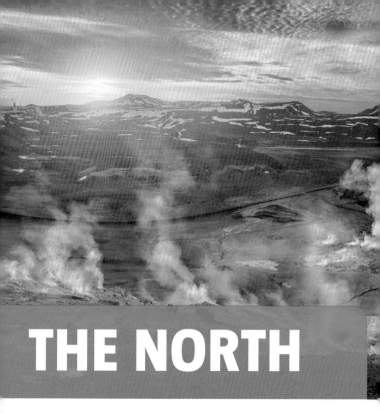

THE NORTH

The northern region is a chequered landscape. One of the most impressive areas in terms of geology and scenery is the Mývatn region.

The main centre of population in the North is Akureyri, a charming little town which has been striving in recent years to turn itself into a mini-metropolis. The many historic sites dotted around Skagafjörður are worth a look. The Skagafjörður region is also famous for horse-breeding.

AKUREYRI

(123 E3) (*M L4*) **Iceland's fourth-largest municipality lies in an attractive spot in the Eyjafjörður region at the foot of** Súlur **(1144 m/1251 ft).** The 18,000 residents live from trade, food production as well as shipbuilding. Akureyri is not only the main tourist centre, but also the cultural heart of the North. Iceland's second university opened its doors to students in 1987. The town owes much of its charm to its many old villas and profusion of trees and is often titled the "Pearl of the North".

SIGHTSEEING

AKUREYRARKIRKJA
A most striking church building for which the architect Guðjón Samúelsson looked to Iceland's typical basalt columns for inspiration. The 17 church windows, illustrating events from the history of Ice-

Hot springs and a wealth of history: the varied face of Iceland's North cannot fail to impress

landic Christianity, are an interesting feature. One window in particular stands out; it was originally part of Coventry Cathedral in England and is 400 years old. *15 June–15 Aug Mon–Thu 10am–4pm | concerts on Sundays in July*

BOTANICAL GARDEN

The Lystigarður garden was laid out in 1912 and is the most northerly of its kind. It contains all of Iceland's native plants (approximately 430 species) and almost 6000 others from various regions, for ex-

ample, Greenland or even Southern Europe. *June–Sept Mon–Fri 8am–10pm, Sat/Sun 9am–10pm | free admission | Eyrarlandsvegur | www.lystigardur.akureyri.is*

DAVÍÐSHÚS

The writer and national poet Davíð Stefánsson (1895–1964) used to live in this house. The rooms look as if he has just left and the library is one of the most valuable private libraries in Iceland. *June–Aug Mon–Fri 1pm–5pm | admission 900 ISK | Bjarkarstígur 6*

HOF CULTURAL AND CONFERENCE CENTRE

It is not only an architectural attraction; it also serves as the tourist information centre. It is the setting for regular exhibitions as well as a varied programme of music and theatre performances. There's also a good restaurant with a terrace di-

BAUTIN

Good restaurant with a nostalgic feel to it and a wide range of dishes. Whale and horse meat specialities and a reasonably priced salad bar. *Hafnarstræti 92 | tel. 4 62 18 18 | Budget–Moderate*

Only 15 m/50 ft high, but still a real stunner: horseshoe-shaped Goðafoss

rectly on the waterfront. Alongside salads, pasta and fish dishes, they also serve cakes. *Strandgata 12 | tel. 4 50 10 00 | www.menningarhus.is | Moderate*

LISTASAFN IN THE LISTAGIL

Three museums were merged together to create the Centre of Visual Arts. Following its refurbishment in 2017/18, the art museum offers even more space for exhibitions of contemporary, Icelandic and international artists. *20 May–Sept daily 10am–5pm, Oct–April Tue–Sun noon–5pm | admission 1500 ISK | Kaupvangsstræti 10 | listak.is | Deiglan is only open for special events*

BLÁA KANNAN

Cosy, popular café in the main shopping street selling snacks and cakes. *Hafnarstræti 96 | tel. 4 61 46 00 | Budget*

SKJALDARVÍK

Bikes for hire from 4 hours (2200 ISK) to several days (3500 ISK a day). For another 2000 ISK, your bike will be brought to the hotel for you. If you prefer being transported on four legs, then book a horse-riding tour, situated roughly 5 km/2 miles to the north of Akureyri at junction 816. *Tel. 552 52 00 | skjaldarvik.is*

HLÍÐARFJALL

Iceland's largest ski resort. A one-day lift pass costs 4900 ISK, and 1-day ski hire 5500 ISK (including helmet and ski sticks). The chairlift operates at the weekends in the summer months (Fri–Sun) and one option is to take a bike up on the lift and hurtle your way back down at top speed. *Tel. 462 22 80 | www.hlidarfjall.is*

AKUREYRI OUTDOOR SWIMMING POOL

Three water slides, a large hot tub with massage jets, a steam bath, sauna and even a place for sunbathing. This pool offers all the standard amenities with its 25 m pool as well as hot pots of varying temperatures. *All year round Mon–Fri 6.45am–9pm, summer Sat/Sun 8am–7.30pm, winter Sat/Sun 9am–6.30pm | 950 ISK, children 6–17: 250 ISK | Þingvallastræti 21 | tel. 461 44 55 | sundlaugar.is*

ÁRSKÓGSSANDI MICROBREWERY

Located 33 km/20 miles north of Akureyri, Bjórböðin ("the beer bath") reminds you of times long ago when rulers would bathe in milk and honey or even in beer foam. You may not believe it but a 25-minute soak in warm beer followed by a chill-out session is the ultimate in relaxation, whether on your own or in a group. *2 persons 14 900 ISK | Ægisgata 31 | tel. 414 28 28 | bjorbodin.is*

WHERE TO STAY

SÆLUHÚS

Surrounded by green fields, 33 bright, modern apartments. Some even have their own hot pot. *Sunnutröð 2 | tel. 618 28 00 | www.saeluhus.is | Moderate*

INFORMATION

TOURIST INFORMATION
Menningarhúsið HOF | Strandgata 12 | tel. 450 10 50 | www.visitakureyri.is

WHERE TO GO

GOÐAFOSS (123 F3) (*M4*)

Some 50 km/31 miles to the east of Akureyri, the Goðafoss waterfall cascades over a broad precipice. It acquired its name "Waterfall of the Gods", in the year 1000, when all statues of the heathen gods were flung into the waters following the adoption of Christianity.

GRÍMSEY (0) (*L1*)

The flight to Iceland's northernmost point takes 20 minutes: the remote island of Grímsey lies on the Arctic Circle (66° 30' North) and is 41 km/25 miles from the mainland. On request, every visitor receives a certificate to document his visit. The towering 100 m/328 ft-high cliffs are a para-

⭐ **Mývatn**
Not only ducks love the lake with its tree-lined banks → p. 66

⭐ **Dettifoss**
Miniature version of the Niagara Falls and the largest waterfall in Iceland → p. 67

⭐ **Jökulsárgljúfur National Park**
It encompasses the gorge carved out by the Jökulsá á Fjöllum river → p. 67

⭐ **Hólar**
Iceland's second bishopric, with the oldest stone church in the country → p. 69

MARCO POLO HIGHLIGHTS

dise for birdwatchers. *Air Iceland | tel. 5 70 30 00 | www.airiceland.is | from 21,000 ISK. From Dalvík, there is a cheaper alternative by boat (see p. 68, low budget)*

MÝVATNSSVEIT

(124 A4) (⟨⟨⟩⟩ M–N 4) The community around Mývatn lake numbers 400 inhabitants. Mývatn, including the largest settlement, Reykjahlíð in the North, is a favourite with tourists.

The Krafla geothermal power plant also plays an important role in the region which is part of an active volcanic zone and experiences frequent eruptions.

SIGHTSEEING

DIMMUBORGIR (124 A4) (⟨⟨⟩⟩ N4)

The lava formations at Dimmuborgir have a fabulous, otherworldly character. Here, you'll come across tunnels and caves with names like *kirkjan,* "The Church". In the summer, you can take a seat on INSIDER TIP "Father Christmas's Chair". Some of the lava sculptures piled up amidst lush vegetation are 40 m/131 ft high. The ⟷ Hverfjall crater to the

north has a diameter of 1 km/0.62 mile and is 140 m/460 ft deep, making it the biggest in Iceland. The entire area is a protected nature reserve.

MÝVATN ★ (124 A4) (⟨⟨⟩⟩ M–N4)

Iceland's fourth-biggest lake is characterised by fascinating lava formations and rich vegetation along its banks. As well as other birds, over 15 species of duck breed here in large colonies, drawn by the favourable climate and plentiful supply of mosquito (larvae), from which the lake takes its name. They may be annoying, but at least they don't bite. Numerous springs issue from the bottom of the lake which has a maximum depth of 5 m/16 ft.

The fine INSIDER TIP *Fuglasafn Sigurgeirs* (Bird Museum) *(mid May–Oct daily noon–5pm, Nov–mid-May 2pm–4pm | admission 1500 ISK | www.fuglasafn.is)*, featuring stuffed specimens of regional birdlife, stands on the north-west bank. The atmosphere in this thoroughly modern showcase, though, is anything but stuffy! ⟷ Café overlooking the lake.

NÁMASKARÐ ● (124 A4) (⟨⟨⟩⟩ N4)

An expanse of solfataras cloaks the base of ⟷ Námafjall (482 m/1581 ft), each

Get close to whales of all kinds on an observation tour off Húsavík

of the many steaming fumeroles belching out sulphur from the springs below. The temperature of the mud pots can reach 100 °C/212°F, and the lighter-coloured parts of the surface crust can cave in easily. Sulphur was extracted here for hundreds of years for use in the manufacture of gunpowder.

FOOD & DRINK

GAMLI BÆRINN (124 A4) (*ω N4*)
The old farmhouse is now a cosy café, serving cakes and light bites. *Reykjahlíð | tel. 4 64 42 70 | Budget*

SPORTS & ACTIVITIES

HIKE AND BIKE
As the name suggests, you can hire bikes (5000 ISK a day) but also book bike excursions or hikes, e.g. a bike and bath tour costs 18,990 ISK. The bike ride around the lake offers plenty of variety in scenery. *Múlavegur 1 | tel. 899 48 45 | hikeandbike.is*

MÝVANT NATURE BATHS
Bathing in turquoise blue, mineral waters surrounded by lava landscape is a dream and there is no nicer place on Mývatn Lake than this lagoon with INSIDER TIP natural baths. *May–June 4700 ISK, July–Sept 5000 ISK, otherwise 4200 ISK | tel. 464 44 11 | myvatnnaturebaths.is*

WHERE TO STAY

SEL-HÓTEL MÝVATN (124 A4) (*ω M4*)
Very well equipped, tastefully furnished and with a view of the lake. Bikes for hire. Plenty of INSIDER TIP activities in winter. *35 rooms | Skútustaðir | tel. 4 64 41 64 | www.myvatn.is | Expensive*

INFORMATION

INFORMATION CENTRE
(124 A4) (*ω N4*)
Hraunvegur 8 | Reykjalíð | tel. 4 64 43 90 | www.visitmyvatn.is

WHERE TO GO

DETTIFOSS ★ (124 B3) (*ω N–O4*)
Around 40 km/25 miles to the north-east of Mývatn, Mother Nature has crafted a gigantic, 100 m/328 ft-wide waterfall. The sheer mass of water from the glacial river Jökulsá á Fjöllum, which plunges 44 m/144 ft into the deep, is such that the surrounding area is enveloped in a cloud of spray lit up by dazzling rainbows.

HÚSAVÍK (123 F1) (*ω M3*)
The main attraction in this prettily situated fishing village, 60 km/37 miles to the north of Mývatn, are the *whale-watching tours (North Sailing | tel. 4 64 72 72| www.northsailing.is)*. The *exhibition* provides in-depth information about all species of whales that live off Iceland's shores. The museum also houses a life-size skeleton of this sea animal. *June–Aug daily 8.30am–6.30pm, May/Sept daily 9am–5pm, Oct/April daily 10am–4pm, Nov–March Mon–Fri 10am–4pm | admission 1900 ISK, children: 500 ISK | Hafnarstétt 1 | tel. 414 28 00 | whalemuseum.is*

JÖKULSÁRGLJÚFUR NATIONAL PARK ★ (124 B3) (*ω N3–4*)
The National Park reaches from Dettifoss – 40 km/25 miles north-east of Mývatn – for over 30 km/18 miles as far as Rte. 85 to the north and is today a part of the large Vatnajökull National Park. The 25 km / 15.5 miles-long and up to 120 m/394 ft-deep *Jökulsárgljúfur canyon*, into which several waterfalls spill their load, is breathtaking.

A hiking trail leads along the gorge to the *Vesturdalur* valley some 16 km/10 miles away. Close by, you'll find the *Hlóðaklettar* basalt formations, nicknamed the "Echoing Rocks". From Vesturdalur, a further day's hike takes you through lush vegetation to *Ásbyrgi* (124 B3) *(ⵎ N3)*, a horseshoe-shaped, thickly wooded ravine with steep sides stretching up almost 100 m/328 ft. There are campsites at Vesturdalur and Ásbyrgi *(tel. 4 70 71 00 | www.vip.is)*.

SAUÐÁKRÓKUR

(126 B2) *(ⵎ H4)* **Would you like to know just how far Grettir, the hero of his own saga, actually swam? You can find out more about this Icelandic outlaw in this region.** The statue of a horse at the entrance to the town shows that you are now entering horse territory. The old town still features many beautiful houses along the Aðalgata. Sauðárkrókur (pop. 2500) is located on the peninsula of Skagi, a good starting point for splendid hikes on the Tindastóll.

LOW BUDGET

The summer concerts in the church in Akureyri are free. Each concert offers a wide range of styles played by talented musicians. It's also a good chance to take in the church, too. *www.akirkja.is*

You can take the ferry to *Grímsey* from Dalvík for just 7000 ISK return. *Mon, Wed, Fri | one-way trip: 3 hrs | tel. 4 58 89 70 | www.saefari.is*

FOOD & DRINK

HARD WOK CAFÉ
The furnishings alone warrant a visit to this establishment which is so tacky it's trendy. Wok dishes are the mainstay but sandwiches and soups are also available. *June–Aug daily 11.30am–9.30pm | Aðalgata 8 | Budget–Moderate*

INFORMATION

TOURIST INFORMATION
In the Minjahús Exhibition Center. *June–Aug daily 1pm–7pm | tel. 4 553618 70 | www.visitskagafjordur.is*

WHERE TO GO

DRANGEY (122 B2) *(ⵎ H3)*
The steep cliffs of the tuff island of Drangey tower some 200 m/656 ft out of the middle of the Skagafjörður fjord. Many species of bird, such as guillemot, build their nests here again today; numbers at the seabird colonies have now recovered. In times of famine – especially in the 18th and 19th centuries – people used to hunt the birds, above all to plunder their nests. In one spring, up to 200,000 birds are said to have been slaughtered. Today, visitors come here only to watch our feathered friends. Information on crossings at the restaurant or the *Reykir* campsite *(departure June–Aug daily 10am | 12,500 ISK | tel. 8 21 00 90 | www.drangey.net)*. In Reykir, you can bathe in the hot Grettislaug springs. *Changing rooms available, 1000 ISK*

GLAUMBÆR (122 C3) *(ⵎ J4)*
Situated 7 km/4.3 miles north of Varmahlíð, this turf farm dating back to the 18th century has now been turned into a museum. Here, you can get an impression of living conditions in such dwell-

ings which were typical for Iceland well into the 19th century. *20 May–Sept daily 9am–6pm | admission 1700 ISK | www.glaumbaer.is*

HOFSÓS (122 C2) *(𝄞 J3)*

It's hard to believe that this sleepy backwater town (33 km/20 miles to the north) was once a hive of activity in the 19th century when thousands of Icelanders waited here in anticipation to sail to the New World. In those days, Hofsós was an important trading centre in Iceland with a large harbour for this period. Some of the emigrants managed to fulfil their dreams in America and Canada but

HÓLAR ★ (122 C3) *(𝄞 J4)*

Iceland's second bishopric (1106–1798) lies 30 km/18.6 miles to the north-east and is also the site of the oldest stone church on the island (1763); the altar features an impressive triptych from the late Middle Ages. Hólar also boasts the first printing press in the country (1530), on which the first Icelandic translation of the Bible was printed in 1584.

The former *Agricultural College* is now a University College specialising in equine science and tourism, aquaculture and fish biology, which are taught in *Sauðárkrókur*. The old school house contains the *Icelandic Horse Centre,* tracing

Not Hobbiton, but Glaumbær: turf houses protect against the Icelandic climate

many returned disappointed. The *Icelandic Emigration Centre* tells the story of these fates and the new lives of the emigrants *(June–Aug daily 11am–6pm | admission 1500 ISK | hofsos.is)*. Another attraction in Hofsós is its spectacular fjord-front swimming pool. Using special floating equipment, it is engulfed in "infinity blue" to mesmerize visitors in the evenings, accompanied by music, midsummer night sun or the northern lights in winter *(daily from 10pm–midnight | 4900 ISK, online registration only using contact form available at infinityblue.is)*

the history of this unique breed. An adjacent building houses a *freshwater aquarium (free admission to both)*. With a number of hiking trails and good places to stay, Hólar is a popular destination in summer. You can stay in cottages and apartments or in sleeping-bag accommodation on the college campus *(Budget–Moderate). Information: campus (tel. 4 55 63 33 | www.visitholar.is). The Centre of the Icelandic Horse, June–15 Sept daily 10am–6pm | admission 1000 ISK | Hóladómkirkja and Nýibær summer daily 10am–6pm, guided tours | holar.is*

THE WEST

Three regions which could hardly be more fascinating make up the West of Iceland. Firstly, there's the area between Borgarnes and Langjökull – with farmland, hot springs, lava caves and lots of places which hark back to saga hero Egill Skallagrímsson.

Further north, the Snæfellsnes Peninsula features the mysterious Snæfellsjökull glacier at its western tip. tip. Today the north coast has just a few larger fishing villages, of which Stykkishólmur is the most important. In the far north-west, the saw-toothed coast of the Westfjords claws the sea; inland, an unparalleled landscape of stark beauty and utter seclusion is a paradise for birdwatchers and hikers. The main town is Ísafjörður, educational and cultural centre of the Westfjords.

BORGARNES

(127 D3) (*∅ E8*) **Despite its ideal location on the sea, the 1800 inhabitants live from trade and processing of agricultural produce.** Hot water emanates from the largest hot-water spring in Iceland, *unguhver*, some 33 km/20 miles away. The town, which was founded in 1867, seems rather sterile. Its charm lies in the fact that you stumble across traces of Egil's Saga Skallagrímssonar everywhere.

SIGHTSEEING

LANDNÁMSSETUR
The museum showcases the story of the settlement of Iceland especially in the

Sagas, beaches and seafarers: on the trail of Egill Skallagrímsson into the bleak, lonely north-west

region around Borgarnes as well the Egil's Saga. Clever use of modern lighting design and good computer animation. *Daily 10am–9pm | admission 2500 ISK, 15–18 years 1900 ISK (for both exhibitions), children free | Brákarbraut 13–15 | www.landnam.is*

SKALLAGRÍMSGARÐUR

This pretty park lies in the centre of town and is the site of the burial mound under which Egill's father, Skallagrímur Kvéldúlfsson, is said to lie. The first settler was laid to rest in the Viking tradition with his horse and weapons. Nearby, a relief shows Egill carrying his drowned son, Böðvar, whom he has also buried under the burial mound, according to the saga.

FOOD & DRINK

BÚÐARKLETTUR

Welcoming restaurant located in an old warehouse directly next to the Settlement Centre. The food's good, too. *Brákarbraut 13–15 | tel. 4 37 16 00 | Moderate*

BORGARNES

Harpoons and oilcloth: the history of whale hunting in the Westfjords museum in Ísafjörður

SPORTS & ACTIVITIES

HVÍTÁTRAVEL

Guided walking tour (in English) for groups on the trail of Egill. *June–Aug | 4200 ISK, 1.5 hours | starting at Landnámssetur Museum (see p. 71) | tel. 6 61 71 73*

ESJA TRAVEL ●

A slightly different Icelandic experience for knitters. The 4-day knitting course in small groups is held in Borgarnes and takes you from the sheep to the scarf. The wool is included in the price. *www. esjatravel.is/en/moya/extras/guided-small-groups/knitting-in-west-iceland*

WHERE TO STAY

BORGARNES HOSTEL

Centrally located hostel with modern furnishings; breakfast as well as a shared kitchen. *19 rooms | Borgarbraut 9–13 | tel. 6 95 33 66 | www.hostel.is | Budget*

INFORMATION

WEST ICELAND TOURIST INFORMATION

In the shopping centre, *Hyrnutorg. Borgarbraut 58–60 | tel. 4 37 22 14 | www.west.is*

WHERE TO GO

BORG Á MÝRUM (127 D3) *(øʊ E8)*

This site, a little to the north of Borgarnes, is where Skallagrímur Kvéldúlfsson and later Snorri Sturluson built their farmsteads. In front of the church, the sculpture Snorratorrek by Ásmundur Sveinsson represents Egill's lament for the death of his son, Böðvar.

HRAUNFOSSAR (127 F2–3) *(øʊ F–G7)*

Some 55 km/34 miles east of Borgarnes, a group of waterfalls, spread over a distance of 1 km/0.62 mile, cascade from the *Hallmundarhraun* lava field. This INSIDER TIP watery spectacle is particularly stunning in September, when the vegetation glows in its autumnal hues.

REYKHOLT ★ (127 E3) *(øʊ F7)*

Today's school and parish centre, 40 km/25 miles to the east, was once home to Snorri Sturluson. An underground passage linked his former house and his ● hot pot, "Snorralaug", and it was here that he was murdered on 22 September 1241. This stone-walled *pool* is one of the few remaining constructions from the Middle Ages. Snorri and further members of his family lie buried at the *cemetery*. The exhibition at the *Snorrastofa* study centre gives an insight into Snorri's works *(May–Aug daily 10am–5pm, Sept–April Mon–Fri 10am–5pm | admission 1200 ISK, with guided tour 2000 ISK | www.snorrastofa.is)*. Programme of classical concerts in the church in summer. A good place to stay is the *Fosshotel Reykholt*, offering a high standard of comfort *(53 rooms | tel. 4 35 12 60 | www.fosshotel.is | Expensive)*.

ÍSAFJÖRÐUR

(120 C2) *(⟡ C3)* **The fishing industry is the main source of income for the 2900 inhabitants of the largest town in the Westfjords region.**

Once the Danish trading monopoly had been relaxed in the 18th century, the town began to flourish. A *seamen's monument* at the cemetery pays tribute to the seafarers who drowned off the coast. A further hint at the close links to the sea is the *whalebone arch* in the park.

SIGHTSEEING

BYGGÐASAFN VESTFJARÐA – WESTFJORDS FOLK MUSEUM
The museum is housed in a former warehouse dating back to the 18th century and documents not only maritime but also municipal history. *15 May–Sept daily 9am–5pm | admission 1300 ISK | Neðstakaupstaður | www.nedsti.is*

FOOD & DRINK

TJÖRUHÚSIÐ
The restaurant on the grounds of the museum is known for its fish buffet. You sit on long tables with benches squeezed into the old "tar house" as its name translates. Book a table in advance. *Daily noon–2pm, 7pm–10pm | Neðstikaupstaður | tel. 4 56 44 19 | Budget–Moderate*

SPORTS & ACTIVITIES

VESTURFERÐIR
Excursions around the region, kayak tours, bicycle hire, riding tours. *Aðalstræti 7 | tel. 4 56 51 11 | www.westtours.is*

WHERE TO STAY

HOTEL EDDA ÍSAFJÖRÐUR
Boarding-school-type accommodation, plus space for sleeping-bag fans and a campsite. *40 rooms | Torfnes school | tel. 4 44 49 60 | www.hoteledda.is | Budget–Moderate*

INFORMATION

TOURIST INFORMATION
At the Edinborg house. *Aðalstræti 7 | tel. 4 50 80 60 | www.isafjordur.is*

MARCO POLO HIGHLIGHTS

★ **Reykholt**
Snorri Sturluson, author and politician, lived here → p. 72

★ **Dynjandi**
Iceland's most beautiful waterfall is close to the coast → p. 74

★ **Látrabjarg**
The country's westernmost cliffs are inhabited by thousands of seabirds → p. 74

★ **Snæfellsjökull National Park**
The famous glacier with the almost magical aura → p. 77

Iceland's most beautiful waterfall: the Dynjandi

miles to the south of Ísafjörður. The water plunges 100 m/328 ft in several fan-shaped cascades. Directly below, there are five more waterfalls, each delightful in its own right. The best view of this waterfall panorama is to be had ⛷ from the coast. Dynjandi – "the thundering one" – is part of a protected nature reserve. You'll find a campsite on the coast.

HORNSTRANDIR
(120–121 C–D1) (*C–D 1–2*)
The 580 km²/224 miles² area in the far north is a hiker's paradise, where the countless abandoned farmhouses – some of them now being re-used as summer holiday cottages – are the only reminder of earlier settlements. Rich vegetation and flocks of seabirds, which nest on the steep cliffs at, for example, INSIDER TIP *Hornbjarg*, are real highlights. Departing from Ísafjörður, the excursions by boat through the nature reserve are a great idea for a day out. Information and tours: *West Tours (tel. 4 56 51 11 | www.westtours.is)*.

LÁTRABJARG ★ ⛷
(120 A4) (*A4*)
The *Bjargtangar* lighthouse, 180 km/120 miles from Ísafjörður, marks the westernmost point in Iceland, and therefore Europe. It stands atop the cliffs of the 14 km/8.7 miles-long Látrabjarg Peninsula, which, at their highest point, tower more than 440 m/1443 ft above the sea. ● Thousands of seabirds nest here; alongside puffins, there is a huge colony of razorbills. A footpath takes you to the picturesque INSIDER TIP *Rauðisandur beach* with its yellowy-red seashell sand. Good accommodation in *Breiðavík*, 13 km/8 miles north of Látrabjarg *(17 rooms | tel. 4 56 15 75 | breidavik.is | Budget–Moderate)*.

DYNJANDI ★ ● (120 C3–4) (*C4*)
This must be Iceland's prettiest waterfall. Also known as *Fjallfoss*, it lies 80 km/50

SKRÍMLISETUR IN BÍLDUDALUR
(120 B4) (ⓜ B4)
120 km/100 miles to the south is where you'll find the sea monster, sightings of which have been reported by the odd local and visitor. The museum explores the secrets of the Icelandic monster in two darkened and eerily decorated rooms. Eye witnesses report of their sightings. The exhibition leaves you thinking there is more to Iceland than elves. After this "encounter", take a relaxing break in the café. *Mid-May–mid-Sept daily 10am–6pm | under tens have to be accompanied by an adult, admission 1000 ISK | Strandgata 7 | tel. 456 66 66 | skrimsli.is*

STYKKIS-HÓLMUR

(126 C1) (ⓜ C–D6) **Thanks to its sheltered harbour, Stykkishólmur was one of the Hanseatic League's trading posts in the 16th century, together with Ísafjördur, Rif, Arnarstapi and Flatey.**
Today's population of 1100 lives mainly from fishing. You can take the "Baldur" ferry from Stykkishólmur to the south coast of the Westfjords.

SIGHTSEEING

SÚGANDISEY ☼
Island which is joined to the mainland by a causeway, thereby offering protection to the harbour. From here, you have a fine view of the islands scattered across the Breiðafjörður bay.

INSIDER TIP VATNASAFN ●
The Library of Water is an installation by the American artist Roni Horn: 24 glass tubes filled with water from Iceland's glaciers, their shimmering colours dictated by the incidence of light. *May–Sept daily 10am–5pm, Oct–April Tue–Sat 10am–5pm | admission 500 ISK | Bókhlöðustigur 17 | www.library ofwater.is*

FOOD & DRINK

NARFEYRARSTOFA
There is a cosy *café (Budget)* on the ground floor of this pretty old house. At the *restaurant (Moderate)* on the first floor you should try the fish soup, made with fish from the fjord. *Aðalgata 3 | tel. 4 38 11 19 | www.narfeyrarstofa.is*

SJAVARPAKKHUSID
Freshly caught and prepared is how fish should be served. This 100-year old fish-packing house is situated directly on the harbour front from where you can watch the comings and goings while enjoying your meal. Old photos remind visitors of former times. The speciality is blue-shell

LOW BUDGET

A wooden crate with regional tomatoes stands next to the island's largest hot water spring, *Deildartunguhver.* They are the cheapest tomatoes in the county at 300–500 ISK per bag. Just drop the money in the box.

The *Sjónarhóll Youth Hostel* is located in one of the oldest buildings in Stykkishólmur, but the rooms have been renovated and are comfy enough. Mostly dormitory accommodation, with a total of 50 beds. *Höfðagata 1 | tel. 4 33 22 00 and 8 61 25 17*

mussels straight from the bay and for dessert make sure to try the Skyr (see p. 28). *Daily noon–10pm | Hafnargata 2 | tel. 438 18 00 | sjavarpakkhusid.is* |Moderate– Expensive

SPORTS & ACTIVITIES

The *Tourist Information Centre* offers guided walking tours through the old part of town. Boat trips, including sea angling, birdwatching or catching some mussels, are run by *Seatours (excursion from 7370 ISK | Smið justígur 3 | tel. 438 22 54 | www.seatours.is).*

SUNDLAUG

Modern swimming pool with special pool for swimmers, slide and hot pots. But the best thing about this pool is the water. With a pH value of 8.45 and high mineral content, the water has rejuvenating powers, ideal for treating psoriasis and other skin diseases or simply for relaxing. Some Icelanders are said to take the water home with them in bottles. *June–Aug Mon–Thu 7.05am–10pm, Fri 7.05am–7pm, Sat/Sun 10am–6pm, Sept–May Mon–Fri 7.05am–10pm, Sat/ Sun 10am–5pm | 900 ISK | Borgarbraut 4 | tel. 433 81 50*

WHERE TO STAY

HORNBJARGSVITI

You can overnight inside the lighthouse at Hornstrandir. A basic, no-frills accommodation with stunning views of blossoming meadows and the sea outside. The next accommodation is 60 km/37 miles away. *fi.is* | Budget

FOSSHOTEL STYKKISHÓLMUR ◌

Situated just outside town on a hill, this hotel offers a restaurant, a great view and comfortable rooms. *79 rooms | Borgarbraut 8 | tel. 430 21 00 | www.islan dshotel.is* | Moderate–Expensivet

THE VIKINGS

Real bad guys, legend has it, who roamed the known world murdering, thieving and pillaging as they went. This image, though, does not tally with that of you're average Icelandic Viking. These were free farmers from Norway who refused to subject themselves to the authority of King Haraldur. Their search for suitable land to settle in brought them to Iceland. Flóki Vilgerðarson set out back in 865 and landed on the north-west coast. He gave the new territory the name Ìsland ("ice land") because he was forced to remain here for two winters, trapped by the ice floes. Despite this hardly flattering designation, word of the land spread quickly, and large-scale settlement began in earnest from 874. The West was much prized by the settlers for its rich pastureland and plentiful fishing grounds. A number of very rich farmers and "Goden , such as Snorri Sturluson, lived here. Some of the best known sagas, too, are set in these parts; *Egil's Saga,* the *Laxdæla Saga* and also the ones about Erik the Red have their origins in this region. It's not surprising, then, that in many places in the West you can come across numerous traces of these saga heroes, the Icelandic Vikings.

TOURIST INFORMATION
In the sports centre. *Borgarbraut 4 | tel. 4 33 81 20 | www.stykkisholmur.is*

WHERE TO GO

EIRÍKSSTAÐIR (127 E1) (*ɰ E6*)
Some 50 km/31 miles west of Stykkishól-mur in the Haukadalur valley at the foot of the Stóra-Vatnshorn lies the birth-place of Leifur Eiríksson. A reconstruction of a longhouse of the 10th century gives an impressive insight into life at the time. Tour guides dressed in medieval costume invite you inside and tell you stories of old times. *June–Aug daily 9am–6pm | admission 1300 ISK | On Rte. 586 | www. eiriksstadir.is*

FLATEY (120 C5) (*ɰ C5*)
Today, the island in the Breiðafjörður is more of a summer stopover, but in the 19th century it was a major cultural centre. "Flat island" became famous due to the Flateyarbók manuscript from the end of the 14th century, which describes, among other things, Leifur Eiríksson's voyage to America. Next to the quaint village and its old houses is a large breeding ground for seabirds. The ● "Baldur" ferry makes for Flatey every day, both from the north-west coast as well as from Stykkishólmur. Information and tickets from *Seatours (see p. 76 | www.seatours.is)*

SNÆFELLSJÖKULL NATIONAL PARK ★ (126 A2) (*ɰ B6–7*)
In the centre of the 167 km²/65 miles² National Park between the villages of Hellnar in the South and Hellissandur in the North, is the 1446 m/4744 ft-high volcanic peak, *Snæfellsjökull*. People believe that the mountain and its immediate surroundings generate a special kind of energy. The

The Malarriff lighthouse watches over the south-western coast of the Snæfellsnes Peninsula

coast at the foot of the volcano is particularly fascinating. Far to the south, the rock pillars at *Lóndrangar,* presumably once magma vents, tower up out of the sea, and out to the west is on the bay of the same name, an important fishing port until the 19th century. All that remains of this once busy settlement are a few ruined buildings and four INSIDER TIP lifting stones of various weights – whoever was not able to lift 49 kg, was not allowed to sign on as a fisherman! The black lava pebble beach at Djúpalónssandur is an attraction in itself.

The *Visitor Center* in Malarrif *(tel. 4 36 68 88 | ust.is/snaefellsjokull-natio nal-park)* informs about nature in the national park and offers guided hikes.

THE HIGHLANDS

The uninhabited Highland region is Iceland at its most primal and breathtaking, a landscape fashioned by volcanic activity and ice. The Hofsjökull and Langjökull glaciers and monumental table mountains, such as the Herðubreið, tower into the sky from the grey-brown lava and gravel plains, dotted with colourful patches of vegetation.

Depending on the weather, the bizarre lava formations seem metamorphosed into menacing figures. For centuries, the two highland routes *Sprengisandsleið* and *Kjalvegur* were the main connection between the North and South, but every traveller was relieved to finally reach his home farm again. The other highland roads were also cross-country riding trails. In the Middle Ages, as a matter of fact, there were also routes across the Vatnajökull glacier – the shortest links between the different regions. These rides, however, were not without their dangers, since numerous outlaws had retreated into the inhospitable Highlands and survived by means of highway robbery. The name of the huge, forbidding lava desert *Ódáðahraun* – which means something like "Evil Deeds Lava" – hints at this fact. Trolls and giants are said to inhabit the region, too...

Today, the rivers and lava fields of the Highlands are a challenge for off-road drivers, mountain bikers and hikers. Almost all trails are well marked, there are a number of mountain huts and campsites, but self-sufficiency is the norm here.

Deserts, mountains and glaciers:
in total silence through the lonely wilderness –
a world away from civilisation

FJALLABAKS-LEIÐ NYRÐI

The "northern trail behind the mountains" runs from west to east and was an essential link for centuries.

The roughly 84 km/52 miles-long route (Rte. F 208) begins in the north-west near the Sigalda power plant on the *Hrauneyalón lake* (128 C3) (*J9*) and ends in the south-east near *Búland* (129 D5) (*K11*), where it joins Rte. 208. Alternatively in the west, follow the Landmannaleið running south for 47 km/29 miles (route F 225). The trail climbs in some places to heights of between 500 and 1000 m (1650 and 3300 ft) and leads through a bizarre, yet beautiful, landscape. To the north of the Hekla volcano, the *Sölvahraun* lava field, with its crevasses and craters, cloaked in black ash, presents an apocalyptic picture.

To the east of the lava fields around Hekla is Iceland's largest area of rhyolite depos-

79

its, covering around 400 km²/155 miles². Rhyolite is a siliceous volcanic rock, notable for its reddish or greenish colour.

ELDGJÁ (129 D4) *(ⓜ K10)*

Translated as the "Fire Gorge", the valley extends for 40 km/25mi from the Uxatindar peak as far as the edge of the Myrdalsjokull glacier in the south-west and looks particularly breathtaking near ✶ *Gjátindur* (935 m/3067 ft) where it is 5 km/3.1 mi long, over 200m/656 ft deep and up to 600 m/1970 ft wide. The oldest

its soothing hot springs. In the "country people's warm springs", the farmers of past centuries used to recuperate from the arduous task of driving their sheep back down the mountains. Today, they are possibly Iceland's best known "bathtub", surrounded by rhyolite peaks. The mountains illuminate in mind-blowing multicolours depending on the position of the sun and air humidity. From ✶ *Bláhnúkur* (943 m/3093 ft) – which gets its name from its blue-green rock – you can look across to the vast obsidian lava field *Laugahraun,* a labyrinthine expanse of black lava formations, some 40 m/131 ft high.

Popular "bathtub" for a chat and a soak: the Landmannalaugar warm springs

lava is around 5000 years old and new layers and currents were added over the years. Some of their lava flows reached as far as the Myrdalssandur sandar plain in South Iceland. The south-westerly section of the Eldgja rift consists of a row of craters.

LANDMANNALAUGAR ★
(128 C4) *(ⓜ J10)*

Like virtually no other place in Iceland, Landmannalaugar is intrinsically linked to

LANDMANNALAUGAR HUT

The Icelandic *Touring Association (Fí)* runs a large mountain hut with a warden and space for up to 78 overnight visitors *(Tel. 8 60 33 35 | Budget)*. Advance booking is essential. There's also a large campsite. From here, the Fí also offers a four-day hike to Þórsmörk along the famous *Laugavegur* trail.

Ferðafélags Íslands (Fí) | Mörkin 6 | Reykjavík | tel. 5 68 25 33 | www.fi.is

KALDIDALUR

(127 F3) *(∅ F–G 7–8)* **Route F 550,** ☼ **the Kaldidalsvegur Route, is only 40 km/25 miles long and runs from Húsafell as far as Rte. 52 near Þingvellir, past the two glaciers, Langjökull and Þórisjökull in the East and the 1198 m/3930 ft-high glacial peak, Ok, in the West.**

Nestled in between the ice, it's easy to see where the place gets its name, climbing as it does to around 700 m/ 2300 ft in some places. The real beauty of the route lies in the views of the glaciers combined with the sight of a number of landmark peaks, such as *Prestahnúkur* (1069 m/3507 ft) which consists of greenish rhyolite rock.

The final destination, *Húsafell,* is one of the Icelanders' favourite places to head for at weekends. Its plentiful coverage of trees and a host of hiking paths mean the area has many weekend cottages and also a large campsite. In the more distant past, the original Húsafell farmstead was an important supply point for travellers on route from North to South. From here, you can undertake excursions to the Langjökull and to the large lava caves, *Surtshellir* and *Stefáns-hellir* **(127 F2)** *(∅ G7)* in the Hallmundarhraun lava field, located to the north of the village on Rte. 518. The road leading there is passable by car; the route is signposted and car parking is available.

Book a tour for an ultimate cave experience which leads you through a lava tube and down into the depths of the cave. It takes you inside the *Víðgelmir* lava cave, with magnificent lava formations in varying sparkling colours to create a magical underground world. *Fljóts-tunga | from 1.5 hrs | 6500 ISK, children 12–15 3500 ISK | www.thecave.is*

Langjökull, Iceland's second largest glacier, welcomes you to step inside. **INSIDER TIP** An artificial tunnel leads you into the ice where you can take a good look at the layers of ice and the world inside an icecap. You can also link the glacier and lava caves (see above), or if not, it's approx. 4 hrs from Húsafell. *19 500 ISK | www.into theglacier.is).* Another exciting adventure is a snowmobile ride on the glacier – ice in all its glory. *From 29,900 ISK*

KJALVEGUR

The imposing highland route, Kjalvegur (Rte. F 35, hire cars not allowed), leads from *Gullfoss* **in the South (128 B2–3)** *(∅ H9)* **165 km/102 miles northwards to the Blanda power plant above the** *Blöndulón* **lake (122 B4)** *(∅ H6).*

Probably the most impressive section of the journey runs through the *Kjölur* valley,

⭐ **Landmannalaugar**
Warm springs surrounded by multi-coloured rhyolite peaks → p. 80

⭐ **Hveravellir**
An oasis for travellers: the thermal area in the middle of the Kjölur valley → p. 82

⭐ **Askja**
Iceland's second-deepest lake, the Öskjuvatn, lies in a stunning caldera → p. 83

⭐ **Kverkfjöll**
Fire and ice – you can't get more Icelandic than this → p. 84

MARCO POLO HIGHLIGHTS

a deserted lava and gravel plain at an altitude of almost 700 m/2300 ft between the Langjökull and Hofsjökull glaciers. Although the journey today is safe and comfortable, it was a far more perilous affair many years ago. The route originally ran further west through the Kjalhraun, but it was re-routed in the wake of a tragic accident in 1780. Four people, together with 180 sheep and 16 horses, died here in a snow storm. To this day, the **INSIDER TIP** *Beinahóll hill* is strewn with animal bones. In this vast expanse of desert terrain, there is no shelter against wind and weather for miles.

SIGHTSEEING

HVERAVELLIR ⭐ (122 C6) (*Ⓜ J7*)

In the middle of the Kjölur, on the northern edge of the Kjalhraun, lies the thermal area of Hveravellir and its bubbling springs and solfataras. There are around 20 springs; some of them stunningly beautiful. *Bláhver*, the 7 m/23 ft-wide "Blue Spring", is characterised by sinter deposits and turquoise-to-aquamarine blue water. The ultimate picture-postcard image is surely *Fagrihver*, the "Beautiful Spring", with its clear, shimmering turquoise waters. In the 18th century, the outlaw Fjalla Eyvindur and his wife hid on the *Kjalhraun*

lava field. The **INSIDER TIP** lava cave – their hideout in the Highlands for 20 years – can still be seen.

KERLINGARFJÖLL (128 C1) (*Ⓜ J8*)

The name Kerlingarfjöll means woman's mountain because it is said that one of the rocks is a female troll set in stone. The myriad colours of the rhyolite mountain ranges towering over the Kjölur plain are visible for miles around. ☀ The highest peaks, Snækollur (1477 m/4846 ft), Loðmundur (1432 m/4698 ft) and Mænir (1355 m/4445 ft) are partially covered with ice caps. The laborious ascent is rewarded with a view reaching from South to North of the island. In some of the multi-coloured, glistening valleys, solfataras make for a steaming, spluttering spectacle.

WHERE TO STAY

HVERAVELLIR (122 C6) (*Ⓜ J7*)

Two huts, open all year round, for up to 53 people. There's also a campsite. Broad range of tours on offer and a natural pool. Bookings: *www.hveravellir.is* | Budget

KERLINGARFJÖLL (128 C1) (*Ⓜ J8*)

Three buildings with 8, 20 and 28 places to sleep, ten cabins with one to four rooms

SUPER JEEPS

Four-wheel vehicles in Iceland are real eye-catchers; with their 44-inch tyres and correspondingly modified, wide bodywork, they look rather intimidating. But when you drive along one of the highland trails yourself, you'll wish you could trade your vehicle for one of these super jeeps. They positively glide over lava, stones and all uneven surfaces. In winter, in particular, their strengths come to the fore, as their thick tyres effortlessly negotiate the snowy surface. These tyres can even be driven at a pressure of 0.1 bar. Consequently, such off-road jeeps are used by rescue services and the fire brigade.

and double room huts. Well-equipped campsite, restaurant and a whirlpool to relax in. *Tel. 6 64 78 78 (in summer)* | *www. kerlingarfjoll.is* | *Budget–Moderate*

ÖSKJULEIÐ

The way to Heaven leads through Hell, so they say: you could certainly say this of this trail (F 88).

edge of the Vatnajökull and the famous Askja caldera.

ASKJA ★ (130 A1) *(∅ N6)*
In the heart of the Dyngjufjöll range, a central volcanic system which has been active for hundreds of thousands of years, lies the Askja caldera with its dazzlingly blue lake, Öskjuvatn. The crater was

A rainbow spans across Bláhver, the "blue spring" in the thermal area of Hveravellir

It leads through ● INSIDER TIP *Ódáðah-raun,* Iceland's largest expanse of lava wasteland, covering 4500 km²/1737 miles² (124 A–B 4–6, 130 A–B 1–2) *(∅ M–O 4–7)*. Lava dating back 5000 years, sand, gravel and monolithic table mountains of palagonite give it its distinctive appearance: black, menacing, dismal and arid. Rainfall seeps away so quickly that plants are unable to make use of the moisture. Only at the edges of the lava desert, green and fruitful oases such as *Herðubreiðarlindir* evolve. Öskjuleið leads over 88 km/55 miles as far as the northern

formed around 6000 years ago and is almost circular, 8 km/5 miles in diameter. Its sides are between 200 and 400 m (655 and 1310 ft) high and are precipitously steep in places. The best view of the Askja is from ⚲ Þorvaldstindur (1510 m/4955 ft) on the southern edge of Dyngjufjöll. The *Öskjuvatn* lake, 217 m/711 ft deep, was the result of a massive eruption in 1875. Ash buried 16 farms and 10,000 km²/3860 miles² of land. On its northern edge lies the crater lake *Víti* with its milky, green-blue water. The last eruption in the Dyngjufjöll was in 1961.

Inside the glacier: melting water has created a cave in the Kverkjökull glacier tongue

HERÐUBREIÐARLINDIR
(124 B6) (*ω O6*)

Lush greenery and over 100 species of plant can be seen in this oasis which forms part of the *Herðubreiðarfriðland* National Park. A striking feature is the abundance of angelica and, after the silence of the lava wastelands, the vibrant sound of birdsong. Some 30 species, most commonly the snow bunting, thrive here. Herðubreiðarlindir takes its name from the formidable ☀ *Herðubreið* mountain (1682 m/ 5518 ft), formed during an eruption under the 1000 m/3280 ft-thick ice crust during the last Ice Age. The ascent is difficult due to the loose covering of scree, but the view from the top is overwhelming.

HÓLUHRAUN (130 A2) (*ω N7*)

This is Iceland's youngest lava – but who knows for how long? You can walk across parts of this newly created, 85 km² (33 mi²) lava field on paths marked by signs. The *Bárðarbunga* volcano on the northwest edge of the Vatnjökull erupted from August 2014 until February 2015.

WHERE TO STAY

DREKI HUT ON DYNGJUFJÖLL
(130 A1) (*ω N6*)

The mountain hut sleeps 55 visitors and is run by Akureyri Touring Club. There is a warden on site and also a campsite. *FFA | Strandgata 23 | Akureyri | tel. 4 62 27 40 and 8 22 51 90 | www.ffa.is | Budget*

WHERE TO GO

KVERKFJÖLL ★
(130 A3) (*ω N8*)

The mountain range on the northern edge of the Vatnajökull, 45 km/28 miles south of the Askja, is a volcanic system with an ice-filled caldera. The glacier tongue *Kverkjökull* pushes its way out of a north-facing opening. One of Iceland's largest geothermal areas lies on the western flank of the range: *Hveradalur*. Here, a series of fascinating ice caves and tunnels have been carved out underneath the glacier.

SPRENGI-SANDSLEIÐ

The 250 km/155 miles-long Sprengisandsleið Route (F 26) runs from the Mýri farm in the North (123 F4) *(ᗰ M5)* **down to the Þjórsárdalur valley in the South** (128 B–C3) *(ᗰ H–J9)*.

It passes through the *Sprengisandur*, Iceland's largest stone desert, stretching from the Hofsjökull to the Tungnafellsjökull glaciers over 70 km/43 miles from north to south. The name, which also designates the route, only came into use in the 18th century. In the Middle Ages, it was simply known as Sandur (sand). The word *sprengir* derives from the verb *sprengja* (to tire out). Sprengisandur was not only feared because of its sandstorms and highwaymen, but also because the individual grazing grounds were more than a day's ride apart. Not surprisingly, riders were keen to reach their destination by nightfall and rode many a horse to death in the process.

SIGHTSEEING

STÖNG (128 B3) *(ᗰ H9)*

Once a large settlement with 20 farmsteads in the fertile Þjórsárdalur valley, Stöng was buried by white volcanic ash in 1104 during one of Hekla's eruptions. Only two farms are left standing today. The indoor ruins can be visited all year round.

HOFSJÖKULL
(122–123 C–D6) *(ᗰ J–K7)*

The third-largest glacier in the country covers an area of 995 km^2/384 miles^2. Its white cap can be seen from miles away and measures up to 1760 m/5774 ft high. It may appear peaceful, but below the summit a volcano slumbers. On the south-

east periphery of the glacier is the *Þjórsárver* Nature Reserve, a swampy area with moorland vegetation, lakes and ponds. Around 11,000 pairs of pink-footed goose nest and rear their young here.

NÝIDALUR (129 E1) *(ᗰ L7)*

This valley on the southern side of the Tungnafellsjökull glacier (800 m/2625 ft) is surprisingly green. You can explore the region from here, e.g. the geothermal area south of the Tungnafellsjökull on the *Eggja* mountain (1271 m/4170 ft).

ALDEYJARFOSS (123 F4) *(ᗰ M5)*

The picturesque Aldeyjarfoss waterfall forms the end point of the Sprengisandsleið where the Skálfandafljót river churns through a narrow passage and into a 20 m deep pool in a canyon lined with basalt column formations. These 4500-year old columns originate from an eruption of the Trölladyngja volcano.

WHERE TO STAY

HERÐUBREIÐARLINDI
(124 B6) *(ᗰ O6)*

Cosiest campsite in the highlands. Sheltered corners can be found; best to stay away from the hut and shower cabins. *Children under 14 free | www.ffa.is | Budget*

LOW BUDGET

Armed with backpack, tent, good hiking maps and several days' rations, your "Hiking in the Highlands" adventure can begin. Deserted landscapes, challenging trails, rivers to wade through – nature at its finest. Countless mountains are just waiting to be climbed, glaciers to be crossed. Often campsites are free.

DISCOVERY TOURS

ICELAND AT A GLANCE

START: ❶ Keflavík END: ㉚ Reykjavík	9 days driving time (without stops) 31 hours
Distance: 🧳 1770 km/1100 miles	

COSTS: 535,000 ISK/2 people (in summer) incl. car hire, petrol, accommodation, food & drink, admission fees
WHAT TO PACK: swimwear, tent, sleeping bag, etc.

IMPORTANT TIPS: Book hotel rooms in advance in summer months. Pay attention to weather reports: avoid travel when storm warnings have been issued *(www.vedur.is)*
Rental cars: only drive where your type of vehicle is permitted.

Along the Ring Road Rte. 1, you can explore the best of what this legendary Nordic island has to offer. This tour takes you to the largest glacier, Vatnajökull, and

Would you like to explore the places that are unique to this region? Then the Discovery Tours are just the thing for you – they include terrific tips for stops worth making, breathtaking places to visit, selected restaurants and fun activities. It's even easier with the Touring App: download the tour with map and route to your smartphone using the QR Code on pages 2/3 or from the website address in the footer below – and you'll never get lost again even when you're offline.

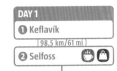

TOURING APP

→ p. 2/3

whisks you away into a magical world of ice and light. Experience the beauty of the deep fjords in the east surrounded by steep mountains and explore the volcanic landscape of the north with its massive waterfalls and historic sites. After this one-of-a-kind encounter with nature, delve into the colourful life of Reykjavik.

As soon as you land, it's time to set off; **the four-lane road from the airport in ❶ Keflavík → p. 113** – Iceland's version of a major motorway – **exit as soon as you see sign No. 1.** Stock up on provisions in **❷ Selfoss → p. 51** – try the regional cheeses – and treat yourself to coffee at **Kaffi-**

DAY 1		
❶ Keflavík		
	98,5 km/61 mi	
❷ Selfoss	☕	🛍

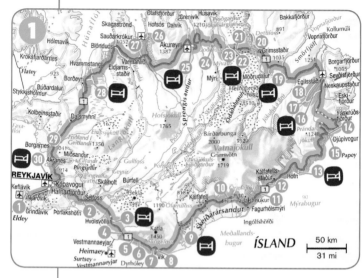

58.5 km / 36 mi

❸ Hellishólar 🍴🏨

31 km / 19 mi

DAY 2

❹ Seljalandsfoss 🌀

19.5 km / 12 mi

❺ Þorvaldseyri Visitor Center 🏛🛍

9.5 km / 6 mi

❻ Skógar 🏛🚶🌳❄

37.5 km / 23 mi

❼ Dyrhólaós

10.5 km / 6.5 mi

❽ Vík í Mýrdal 🚶🛍

79 km / 49 mi

Krús → p. 51. Drive past lush green meadows as you **pass through Hvolsvöllur** and into a snug dale on the way to ❸ Hellishólar *(www.hellisholar.is)*. In addition to a restaurant, there are also cabins and camping facilities available.

Follow the attractive country road **over the glacial river of Markarfjót and continue on** to the 40 metre-high (130 ft) waterfall ❹ Seljalandsfoss. If you'd like, you can walk behind the waterfall. At ❺ Þorvaldseyri Visitor Centre *(www.icelanderupts.is)*, the eruption of Eyjafjallajökull in 2010 is brought back to life – for a unique souvenir, check out the **INSIDER TIP** ash soap sold here. In ❻ Skógar → p. 53, visit the regional museum **Skógasafn**, which offers a comprehensive view of what life was like in 19th-century Iceland. Top off this stop on the tour with a walk to the **Skógafoss** waterfall. The platform above the falls offers a lovely view of the coast and the tumbling water. **Continue driving over the Sander plains to turn-off No. 215,** which leads to one of Iceland's most beautiful beaches. Black lava pebbles and a cave made of basalt formations await along the estuary of ❼ Dyrhólaós. ❽ Vík í Mýrdal → p. 52 is located within **Katla Geopark**, and you can walk along the beach as far as the three **Reynisdrangar** sea stacks. Fans of classic Nordic jumpers should make sure to check out the large selection of hand-knit clothing at **Ice**

Wear (*Austurvegur 20*). Spend the night at a camping pitch in ⑨ **Kirkjubæjarklaustur**.

Get an early start on the third day. The route over the dark Sander at the foot of Vatnajökull is quite impressive. In ⑩ **Skaftafell** → p. 61, hike to the picturesque waterfall of **Svartifoss** → p. 61 with its basalt formations **(round trip 1 hr.)** and then to the glacier tongue of **Skaftafellsjökull** → p. 61. The exhibit in the **visitor's centre** describes the Vatnajökull National Park as well as how the glacier is continually receding. The next highlight is the lagoon of ⑪ **Jökulsárlón** → p. 61. Blue, white and black icebergs float on the water, which you can also walk along. The path to the coast is also stunning, but it can be quite overcrowded during the peak season. As you head east from Jökulsárlón, you'll encounter mesmerizing views of the Vatnajökull. In ⑫ **Hali** → p. 60, it's worthwhile checking out the **museum** honouring the poet Þórbergur Þórðarson with its adjacent restaurant. After a dose of culture and a good meal, drive to ⑬ **Höfn** → p. 59 and spend the night at the prettily situated **Edda-Hotel** → p. 60.

The **regional museum** → p. 60 in Höfn provides a glimpse into the life of the fishermen. Take one final look at the Vatnajökull **before steering towards the fjords along the east coast.** Geologically-speaking, the mountain ranges here count among the oldest features of the country and the fjords have carved deep into the rock. As you drive along, admire the wonderfully beautiful views of the colourful rhyolite mountains as in Lón. In ⑭ **Djúpivogur** → p. 54, an amusing art installation made of oversized stone eggs adorns the quay. An ideal place to go for lunch is the ⑮ **Langabuð Café** in the village of the same name where the menu usually features a good soup and salad. **At Breidalsvík, you'll turn away from the coast and drive up through some narrow valleys. Before you get to Egilsstaðir, turn onto Rte. 931** so you can sleep in the forest of Hallormsstaður at Lake Lagarfljót in ⑯ **Hotel Hallormsstaður** → p. 58.

The route around the **Lagarfljót → p. 58**, which is really only a broad stretch of river, will take you through Iceland's largest forest, **Hallormstaðurskógur** → p. 58, and then on to ⑰ **Skriðuklaustur** → p. 58. The town is not only of historical and cultural significance, but also it is a

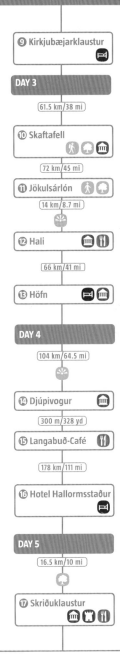

⑨ Kirkjubæjarklaustur

DAY 3

61.5 km/38 mi

⑩ Skaftafell

72 km/45 mi

⑪ Jökulsárlón

14 km/8.7 mi

⑫ Hali

66 km/41 mi

⑬ Höfn

DAY 4

104 km/64.5 mi

⑭ Djúpivogur

300 m/328 yd

⑮ Langabuð-Café

178 km/111 mi

⑯ Hotel Hallormsstaður

DAY 5

16.5 km/10 mi

⑰ Skriðuklaustur

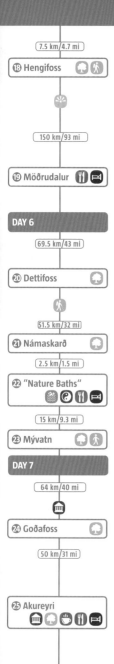

7.5 km / 4.7 mi

⑱ Hengifoss

150 km / 93 mi

⑲ Möðrudalur

DAY 6

69.5 km / 43 mi

⑳ Dettifoss

51.5 km / 32 mi

㉑ Námaskarð

2.5 km / 1.5 mi

㉒ "Nature Baths"

15 km / 9.3 mi

㉓ Mývatn

DAY 7

64 km / 40 mi

㉔ Goðafoss

50 km / 31 mi

㉕ Akureyri

good place to have lunch in the **INSIDER TIP** cafeteria. The excellent dishes feature regional products. **A bit further to the north, you'll come to the starting point for a hike (round trip 2 hrs.) to** ⑱ **Hengifoss**. This waterfall is surrounded by basalt rock formations. **Follow Rte. 931 back to Rte. 1, and head west** as you enjoy the ever more beautiful views of the highlands. **Turn off onto the old ring road (Rte. 901)** because it offers the best taste of the landscape. The mesa of Herðubreið → p. 84 will arise before you off into the distance. Spend the night at the former farm ⑲ **Möðrudalur** that has been converted into an inn with a camping pitch.

Lava dominates the landscape in this area – the original face of Iceland. **Rte. 862 runs** to the country's largest waterfall, ⑳ **Dettifoss** → p. 67. You won't regret **hiking for a bit to the north from here** to admire the start of the Jökulsárgljúfur canyon and the Hafragilsfoss waterfall. **Afterward, head back to Rte. 1.** You'll see the steam of the next stop as you approach, and depending on the winds, you might also smell its sulphurous odour ㉑ **Námaskarð** → p. 66 is a thermal area with numerous bubbling and hissing springs. The steam rises on the other side of the pass as well, but now it's time to relax and enjoy the ㉒ **Nature Baths** → p. 67. Check into your small cabin at **Hlíð Ferðaþjónusta** *(myvatnaccommodation.is)* for the night and spend the evening on lake ㉓ **Mývatn** → p. 66 near **Kálfaströnd** on the south east coast and bask in the light of the midnight sun on a walk through the **Dimmuborgir** → p. 66.

Lake Mývatn is a paradise for bird-lovers. If you don't manage to see all the varieties out in their natural habitat, you can head to the **Bird Museum** → p. 66. The next highlight of the tour is ㉔ **Goðafoss** → p. 65, the waterfall of the gods, **which is located directly on Rte. 1.** Streams cascade over the rocks, creating an imposing wall of water. Having now experienced the natural beauty of the country, it's time to check out its cities and culture. A lovely place to stay in ㉕ **Akureyri** → p. 62 is **Sæluhús** → p. 65, and you can easily explore the city on foot. Discover contemporary Icelandic art at the **Art Museum** → p. 64 and stroll through the country's varied plant life on display in the **Botanical Garden** → p. 63. The adjacent small **café** is a good place to take a break. Don't miss out on a visit to the **Hof Cultural and Conference Centre** → p. 64. Its **restaurant** fea-

Magical colours: black, turquoise and blue icebergs float in the glacial lake of Jökulsárlón

turing a view of the fjord and the mountains is a good place to wind down in the evening.

On Day 8, the route starts in the mountains whose impressive ragged peaks jut into the sky. At the end of the narrow valley, the landscape spreads out again **as you follow Rte. 76 to the north** to the former bishop's residence of ㉖ **Hólar → p. 69**. After a tour and a bite to eat, **drive back and then take Rte. 1 and Rte. 75 to** ㉗ **Glaumbær → p. 68**, one of the prettiest turf farms in the country. Merely the view from the outside makes a stop worthwhile. Be sure to try some of the Icelandic baked goods served in the café. Plan to spend the night **about 55 km (34 miles) further to the southeast of Blönduós** with its **textile museum** on the horse farm ㉘ **Brekkulækur → p. 102**. The owners can tell you a lot about the country and its people, but most especially about its horses.

After leaving this mostly agricultural area, you will come to a plateau where you can see some of the glaciers in the highlands, such as Eiríksjökull, on clear days. The landscape is marked by lava of different ages, dotted

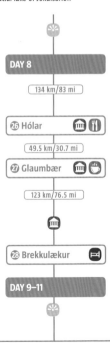

DAY 8

134 km / 83 mi

㉖ Hólar

49.5 km / 30.7 mi

㉗ Glaumbær

123 km / 76.5 mi

㉘ Brekkulækur

DAY 9–11

121 km/75 mi

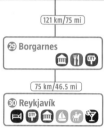

㉙ Borgarnes

75 km/46.5 mi

㉚ Reykjavík

here and there with small, fenced-in reforestation areas and striking crater mounds. ㉙ Borgarnes → p. 70 is a legendary place, even though its rather sterile appearance would seem to suggest otherwise. At the Landnámssetur → p. 70, delve into the history of the area's settlement and Egil's Saga. After lunch in Búðarklettur → p. 71, take a look at some of the saga sites. Then, steer for ㉚ Reykjavík → p. 32, where you can spend the night in one of the city's many hotels.

The new landmark of Reykjavík is the concert hall called Harpa → p. 36 with its impressive facade and interior design. Perlan → p. 36, the domed building that you can see from afar, offers the best view of the city and its surroundings from the viewing deck. You can't miss out on a walk through the historic city centre and a visit to the Harbour House → p. 35 – simply a must for art lovers – as well as a stroll along Laugavegur → p. 39, which is lined by inviting cafés and restaurants. If you're interested in marine life, take a whale-watching tour and/or check out the whale museum → p. 106. You can also book a short horseback ride at Íshestar stables → p. 102 (they will pick you up). In the evening, head out to the bars in the city centre.

2 NATURE AND CULTURE: THE GOLDEN CIRCLE

START: ① Reykjavík	3 days
END: ① Reykjavík	driving time
Distance:	(without stops)
275 km/170 miles	6 hours

COSTS: 110,000 ISK/2 people incl. car hire, petrol, accommodation, food & drink, admission fees, spa visit
45 min. diving tour 15,000 ISK/person
WHAT TO PACK: swimwear

IMPORTANT TIPS: Book hotel rooms in advance in summer months. Pay attention to weather reports: avoid travel when storm warnings have been issued (www.vedur.is)
Rental cars: only drive where your type of vehicle is permitted. Book diving tour in advance and confirm location: www.divesilfra.is

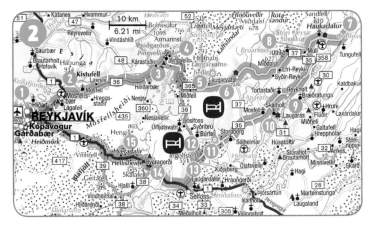

The Golden Circle is one of Iceland's most popular tours, offering an impressive mix of culture, history and nature. Take you time and plan in some walks to explore the different stops at your leisure.

Take Rte. 1 from ❶ Reykjavík → p. 32 heading north to Mosfellsbær. Just as you leave the village, turn off onto Rte. 36, the Þingvallavegur. After a few kilometres, you will come to ❷ Gljúfrasteinn *(June–Aug. daily 9am–5pm | www.gljufrasteinn.is)*, the former house of the Noble-prize wining author Halldór Laxness, who lived here with his family after 1945. This house full of history has now been turned into a museum. When you are up on the plateau of Mosfellsheiði, you'll be able to see Iceland's largest lake, ❸ Þingvallavatn → p. 43, and the adjoining National Park ❹ Þingvellir → p. 43. The observation point at the Information Centre offers a sweeping view into the highlands. Numerous signposted trails lead from here to Lögberg, through the Almannagjá and further on to Öxará Waterfall. A snorkelling or diving excursion in the Silfra Rift → p. 43 is a spectacular way to get acquainted with the lake and the geology of the park.

The route continues on through a scrub forest near the lake **and then towards Laugarvatn via Rte. 365.** You'll drive over the foothills of an extinct shield volcano in a landscape full of different kinds of lava. **Halfway to the next destination,** you'll come across the two caves of ❺ Laugarvatnshellir, which were still inhabited at the beginning of the 20th century! The village of ❻ Laugarvatn with its

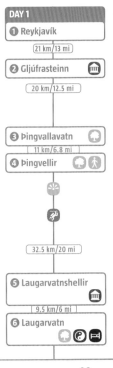

DAY 1

❶ Reykjavík

21 km / 13 mi

❷ Gljúfrasteinn

20 km / 12.5 mi

❸ Þingvallavatn

11 km / 6.8 mi

❹ Þingvellir

32.5 km / 20 mi

❺ Laugarvatnshellir

9.5 km / 6 mi

❻ Laugarvatn

forests and holiday cottages is a popular choice for a short getaway during the summer months. The hot springs are mostly used to heat greenhouses. The **Golden Circle Apartments** *(25 apts. | Laugarbraut 1 | tel. 4 87 12 12 | www.gold-encircleapartments.is | Expensive)* situated close to the lake and the wonderful "Hot Pots" of the **Fontana Spa** *(Hverabraut 1 | Tel. 4 86 14 00 | www.fontana.is)* are an ideal place for a relaxing stay. Here you can get a 10% discount if you show your apartment key.

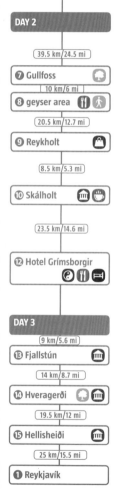

DAY 2

39.5 km / 24.5 mi

7 Gullfoss

10 km / 6 mi

8 geyser area

20.5 km / 12.7 mi

9 Reykholt

8.5 km / 5.3 mi

10 Skálholt

23.5 km / 14.6 mi

12 Hotel Grímsborgir

DAY 3

9 km / 5.6 mi

13 Fjallstún

14 km / 8.7 mi

14 Hveragerði

19.5 km / 12 mi

15 Hellisheiði

25 km / 15.5 mi

1 Reykjavík

Head northeast via Rte. 37 and Rte. 35 into the thermal geyser area around Haukadalur – which you can see from afar thanks to the fountain of water spewed by the Strokkur geyser → p. 51. Continue driving on to the impressive waterfall **7 Gullfoss** → p. 52. **Several paths lead closer to the cascades. Return to the 8 geyser area**, where you can explore the hot springs at your leisure. **Afterwards, continue driving to the south.** The small village of **9 Reykholt** → p. 73 is home to numerous greenhouses heated with the steaming hot water that you can see from afar. Pay attention to the signs on the side of the road for places to **INSIDER TIP** buy fresh tomatoes and strawberries (cheap and tasty). **A few kilometres further on, Rte. 31 branches off** to the Bishop's seat of **10 Skálholt**, which was the cultural centre of Iceland from the Middle Ages into the 19th century. Treat yourself to some home-made cake in **the school building** before heading **southward on Rte. 35. After 18 km,** you will come to the 3,000 year-old and 55 metre-deep explosion crater filled with water on the left called **11 Kerið. Then turn right onto Rte. 36** and wind down for the evening at **12 Hotel Grímsborgir** → p. 51 with a bath in a "Hot Pot" and a gourmet dinner.

Shortly before you come to the ring road leading to Reykjavík, stop briefly at **13 Fjallstún** at the foot of the Ingólfs-fjall, supposedly the site where the first settler of Iceland, Ingólfur Arnarson, spent his first winter. You should also stop at **14 Hveragerði** → p. 47 to visit the geothermal field. The **exhibition** in the shopping centre shows the damage caused by the earthquake in 2008. At the geothermal power plant **15 Hellisheiði** *(daily 9am–5pm | www.on-power.is)*, you can learn about the uses of geothermal energy as well as the history of the region with its many legends **before you make your way back to 1 Reykjavík** → p. 32.

3
SKIRTING THE GLACIER: KJALVEGUR

START: ❶ "Hvítarvatn" END: ❼ Hveravellir	4 days walking time (without stops) 16 hours
Distance: ➡ 51 km/32 miles	Difficulty: ▂▃▄ easy

COSTS: bus tickets 12,000 ISK/person, cabins 5,000 ISK per person per night

WHAT TO PACK: tent, backpack, food & drink, trail maps, sleeping bag, etc.

IMPORTANT TIPS: Book and pay for cabins in advance *(www.fi.is)*; you'll still need a sleeping bag, rations, and waterproof gear. Up-to-date trail maps are sold at tourist information centres or bookshops in Reykjavík.
Buses run daily in summer from Reykjavík and Akureyri over the mountain track Kjölur. Tell the driver that you want to get off in Hvítárnes when you board the bus.

On this hiking tour, experience the natural beauty of Iceland in typical Icelandic fashion: the path is the true destination. This route is also ideal for inexperienced hikers because the stages are relatively short without many climbs and the trails at the foot of Langjökull through the lava landscapre are well marked.

This route begins at the sign for ❶ **"Hvítarvatn"** on the jeep track Kjölur, **where you'll get off the bus and walk to the ❷ Hvítárnes lodge**. This red-roofed lodge is located on Lake Hvítárvatn on the eastern edge of the Langjökull. From here you can see the Nyr-ðriskriðjökull glacier, which used to calve into the lake. Next to the lodge dating back to 1930, you will see the ruins of a farm. Settlers appear to have put down roots here in the 9th century because the lake had a good stock of fish. Nowadays, the area is a paradise for bird-watchers thanks to the many INSIDER TIP species of bird to be found here.

On the morning of the second day, get your bearings by following the stone cairns to the east of the lodge that mark the way to the old Kjalvegur → p. 81. **The path leading northeast along the river Fúlakvísl is easy to follow.** The rich vegetation surrounding the tuff mound ❸ **Hrefnubuðir** comes as a surprise and there are even

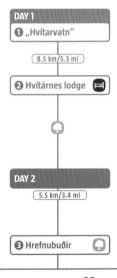

DAY 1
❶ „Hvítarvatn"

8.5 km/5.3 mi

❷ Hvítárnes lodge

DAY 2

5.5 km/3.4 mi

❸ Hrefnubuðir

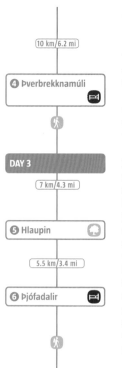

Warm water in a wild landscape:
Hot Pot in Hveravellir

10 km/6.2 mi

4 Þverbrekknamúli 🏠

🚶

DAY 3

7 km/4.3 mi

5 Hlaupin 🎧

5.5 km/3.4 mi

6 Þjófadalir 🏠

🚶

birch trees growing here at an elevation 400–500 metres (1,300– 1,640 ft). The mesa of Hrútfell (1410 m/4625 ft) provides orientation from a distance whilst the Kerlingarfjöll Mountains → p. 52 rise up to the east. Once you have crossed the Þverbrekknaver marsh, **cross the bridge over the river and follow the posts to 4 Þverbrekknamúli.** Pretty tent pitches are situated along the stream not far from the lodge. You can also embark on a mountain hike to the **Fjallkirkja** rock formation on the Langjökull about 15 km (9 miles) away from here.

Head back to the bridge and continue along the old Kjalvegur. Since you will not cross any more rivers, make sure to stock up on INSIDERTIP▶ water from the streams at the lodge. **At first, the trail runs parallel to the small Fúlakvísl river,** which flows into a narrow canyon. **Then it runs to the east of the hill Múli** before coming to the narrow **5 Hlaupin** canyon, where the Fúlakvísl once again tumbles through the lava rock. **Keep your bearings as you walk north by heading towards Þjófafell (960 m/3150 ft).** Follow along the green banks of the stream Þjófadalaá to the valley of **6 Þjófadalir** to the west of the mountain, which is home to the next lodge. In days gone by, the secluded valley was a hideaway for highwaymen, earning its name as "thieves' valley". From here, you can also tag on a day's hike to the Rauðkollur (1060 m/3480 ft) to see more glaciers.

On day 4, hike to Þröskuldur pass, **where you will come across the jeep route F 735 to Hveravellir, as this enticing trail runs further to the southeast.** In ➐ Hveravellir → p. 82, you can recover from the hike with a bath in the thermal spring water, but make sure to shower first! The well-equipped **camping pitch** has a lodge as well as a small **cafeteria,** but you should also check out the **geothermal site** and take the time for a tour.

DAY 4
14.5 km/9 mi
➐ Hveravellir
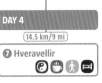

4 CAPTIVATING WILDERNESS: ÖSKJULEIÐ

START: ❶ Mývatn	2 days
END: ❾ Holuhraun	driving time
Distance:	(without stops)
➡ 170 km/106 miles	5.5 hours

COSTS: 48,000 ISK/2 people incl. jeep rental, petrol, accommodation
WHAT TO PACK: tent, food & drink, swimwear, sleeping bag, etc.

IMPORTANT TIPS: Book and pay for cabins in advance *(www.fi.is)*
Pay attention to weather reports: avoid travel when storm warnings have been issued *(www.vedur.is)*
Be sure to wear hiking boots even when driving.
Try only to ford waterways together with other vehicles. Be careful where you cross. In the water, steer against the current. The earlier you start in the day, the lower the water levels in the rivers.

This highland route is one of the loveliest, passing through the black-grey lava desert of Ódáðahraun. The unique landscape is definitely a challenge for whoever is driving, making the trip adventurous for many. You'll travel to green oases, discover one of Iceland's most impressive natural monuments, Askja, and dive into a newly formed lake.

Start off from ❶ Mývatn → p. 66. **The jeep track F 88 begins about 40 km (25 miles) to the east.** You'll soon come across the ❷ Hrossaborg crater whose partially collapsed rim towers up 40 m (130 ft) – if you want, you can also climb to the top. **Continue driving, parallel to the glacial river Jökulsá á Fjöllum.** The river begins at the Vatnajökull, which you will only see from afar at a few points along this route. **Ford for the first time across the** ❸ Grafarlandaá, which marks the boundary of a nature conservation area covering 170 km² (65 mi²) as

DAY 1
❶ Mývatn
36 km/22.4 mi
❷ Hrossaborg
38.5 km/24 mi
❸ Grafarlandaá

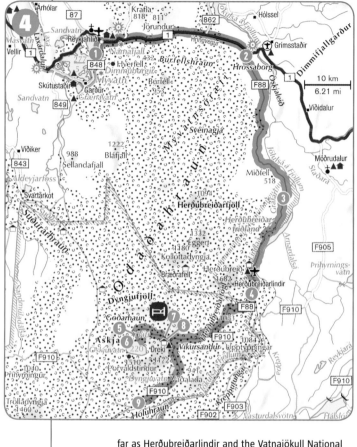

20 km/12.4 mi

4 Herðubreiðarlindir

far as Herðubreiðarlindir and the Vatnajökull National Park. Before you reach this pretty spot with its bubbling streams and rich vegetation, **you still have to drive through the Lindaá river.** At the oasis of **4** Herðubreiðarlindir → p. 83, you should stop and head to the nearby INSIDER TIP lava field formed by a pāhoehoe lava flow. This rock formation resembling side-by-side ropes is created when layers of thin, low-gas lava are successively shoved together. Take a look at the spot where Iceland's legendary outlaw, Fjalla-Eyvindur ("Eyvindur from the mountains"), supposedly spent the winter of 1774/75.

The journey continues past the 8 km (5 mile) long tuff ridge Herðubreiðartögl (1059 m/3474 ft) south of Herðubreið mountain. The ground here consists largely of pale pumice formations whose ash is carried for hundreds of kilometres by the stormy winds. The next destination is the Dyngjufjöll volcano with its peak rising 600–700 m (1970–2300 ft) above the surrounding area, and its caldera Askja → p. 83. On the northern rim of the caldera, you will find the explosion crater ❺ **Víti** and the milky water of lake ❻ **Öskjuvatn**. When you walk from Víti to the northern edge of Öskjuvatn, you will pass a monument to a German geologist and his friend who disappeared at the lake in 1907. Return to the car park and head on back to the camping pitch at the lodge ❼ **Dreki**, where you can spend the night. By the way, the lava along the way was used as a training site for astronauts in 1968.

After a good night's sleep, it's worth the effort to walk through ❽ **Drekagil** gorge with its bizarre lava formations resembling dragons' heads. At the end is a magnificent waterfall. The entrance to the gorge lies behind Dreki lodge. Depart Dreki to the south on the F 910, past the shield volcano Vaðalda and Dyngjuvatn lake, until you come to the INSIDERTIP "new lava" of ❾ **Holuhraun**. It was spewed when the Bárðarbunga volcano erupted for eight months until early 2015. The lava field covers an area of 85 km² (33 mi²), and signs indicate the areas of the lava field where you are permitted to walk. As you head back north after a stroll, you will surely be delighted by the new views and all the things you can see from this change in perspective.

44 km/27 mi

❺ Víti

1 km/0.6 mi

❻ Öskjuvatn

10.5 km/6.5 mi

❼ Dreki

DAY 2

❽ Drekagil

19 km/11.8 mi

❾ Holuhraun

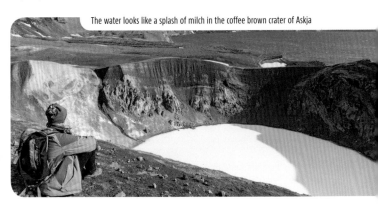

The water looks like a splash of milch in the coffee brown crater of Askja

SPORTS & ACTIVITIES

The many outdoor activities on offer are an ideal way to get to know and appreciate Iceland's countryside. The horse was once the most reliable means of transport in Iceland. Today, most Icelanders ride for pleasure and the favourite pastime of many Reykjavík locals is spending their Sundays at the riding stables with their horses and their families.

Swimming is a national institution and an essential skill for children to learn. In recent years, hiking and golf have been discovered by an ever-wider audience.

advice from local hiking guides, too. If you are attempting such a tour for the first time, the excursions offered by the Icelandic touring associations are an ideal alternative. Instead, you could also opt for a ride in a jeep or on a snowmobile across the glaciers, as offered by tour operators in Reykjavík and Höfn. A good source of information and operator of tours – especially on the Vatnajökull – are the *Icelandic Mountain Guides (Bankastræti 2 | Reykjavík | tel. 5 87 99 99 | www.mountainguides.is)*

GLACIER TOURS

Experienced ice climbers can undertake solo tours across the Langjökull or the Vatnajökull, but it is still important to get

GOLF

There are 65 golf courses in the country, and some greens have been intriguingly incorporated into the lava landscape. Most

In the water or on land, on glaciers or at the lakes: there's a host of things to do in the great Icelandic outdoors

courses are open to foreign visitors for a reasonable green fee. Golf is a sport for all the family in Iceland so make sure to pack your putters *(golficeland.org)*.

HIKING

The Highlands and the north-west and north-east of Iceland offer hikers solitude and some intense encounters with nature. Some of the trails are well marked and very popular; others you can discover under your own steam. The main prerequi-

site for a multiday trek is good physical shape and the right equipment, as you must reckon on experiencing all kinds of weather. Good hiking maps and guides for the most popular routes are available from most bookshops in Reykjavík. One-day walks, e.g. on Hekla or around Skaftafell, are also a great way to see the countryside. To make the most of the experience, though, you need to be prepared to cope with the extremely changeable weather and have suitable clothing, footwear and sufficient provisions. Organised tours of varying degrees of difficulty are offered by the two Icelandic *touring associations* (see "Mountaineering") and *Icelandic Mountain Guides* in Reykjavík (see "Glacier Tours"). Ideal for families: tours guided by INSIDER TIP *wanderlust (www.wanderlust.is),* sometimes with picnic. The guided walks in Höfn with tour guide Hulda are a very relaxing and intimate experience *(hof nlocalguide.com)*

HORSE RIDING

Riding opportunities range from one-hour rides – also for complete beginners – to highland tours lasting several weeks, with two horses per rider. *Íshestar* in *Hafnarfjörður* offers short horseback excursions *(tel. 5 55 70 00 | www.ishestar.is).*

Arinbjörn Jóhannsson at *Brekkulækur farm (Brekkulækur | tel. 4 51 29 38 | www. abbi-island.is)* will help you get to know the Arnarvatnsheiði plateau in connection with fishing and birdwatching – the ultimate, back-to-nature experience. Other horseriding stables can be found in the *Hey Iceland* brochure "Self-Drive in Iceland" where farms with horseriding facilities are marked *(heyiceland.is/about-us/ brochures).* Riding equipment must be disinfected before entering the country!

KAYAK

Experienced kayakers can explore all of Iceland. Kayak tours into the fjords or on the Heinabergslón glacier lagoon are spectacular and both can be done in summer. You can silently cut through the waters to the icebergs *(iceguide.is/tours)*

MARATHON

Iceland offers some fantastic routes for long-distance runners. The Reykjavík Marathon takes place every year on August 20. The classic 55 km/34 mile hiking route from Landmannalaugar to Þorsmörk is used for the Laugevegur Ultra Marathon. The Suzuki midnight sun race held in Reykjavík in June offers participants the opportunity to choose one of three different distances: a half-marathon, 10 km/6 miles and 5 km/3 miles. But you can register to take part in all three distances. At the end of May/beginning of June is the Mývatn Marathon. *Registration: marathon.is, myvatnmarathon.com*

MOUNTAIN BIKING

If you couldn't fit your mountain bike in your suitcase, you can hire one in Reykjavík and in a number of other towns and villages. The routes along the coast near Reykjavík or around the Mývatn lake are beautiful and ideal for hobby cyclists. Tourist information offices have lists of places to hire mountain bikes and book guided tours. Information: *Icelandic Mountain Bike Club (www.fjallahjolak lubburinn.is)*

MOUNTAINEERING

The many mountains are an open invitation to climbing enthusiasts, but the prevalence of loose surface rock and the sudden changes in the weather mean that individual tours are only to be recommended for experienced mountaineers. Essential equipment on any mountain excursion should include emergency rations and first-aid kit, plus a bivouac sack and emergency foil blanket. The Icelandic touring associations also offer guided tours. Both have their headquarters in *Reykjavík: Ferðafélag Íslands (Mörkin 6 | tel. 5 68 25 33 | www.fi.is); Útivist (Laugavegur 178 | tel. 5 62 10 00 | www. utivist.is).*

Adventure in the saddle: mountain bikers on the Kjölur Route

RAFTING

Fun for all the family at several locations on the larger glacial rivers. Operators include, for example, *Arctic Rafting (Reykjavík | Laugavegur 11 | tel. 5 71 22 00 | www.arcticrafting.is)* in the South and, in the North in *Varmahlíð, Activity Tours (tel. 4 53 83 83 | www.activitytours.is)*

STAND-UP PADDLING

A sport destined for Iceland! A popular spot for paddling is þingvallavatn Lake, Iceland's largest lake. Another lake suitable for SUP is Hvalfjörður. The stand-up paddle board and all the gear are provided *(adventurevikings.is)*

SWIMMING

Swimming is the national sport. Once you've tried the warm waters of the open-air swimming pools, you're sure to be hooked. In Reykjavík alone there are seven pools, and several more in the surrounding villages. Here in particular, efforts have been made to upgrade facilities, a fact which makes these the ideal spot for a family day out. Every large town or village has an open-air swimming pool.

WELLNESS

The spa oases in Iceland are the Blue Lagoon or the Nature Bath on Mývatn. Hotels in Reykjavík as well as large hotels in the country also offer spa treatments.

WINTER SPORT

In winter, both cross-country and downhill skiing are possible. There are ski resorts at, for example, *Bláfjöll* south of Reykjavík or above Akureyri on *Hlíðarfjall*. Snow conditions permitting, you can undertake attractive cross-country tours all over the island; the Icelanders' favourite areas are the INSIDER TIP north-west and the Mývatn area. In addition, you could try one of the Ski-Doo snowmobile tours on signposted routes.

TRAVEL WITH KIDS

Icelanders have a decidedly relaxed and uncomplicated attitude towards children. Families are very close-knit; looking after the children is a task shared by all members, and kids, parents and grandparents generally never live far away from each other.

The number of young mothers is comparatively high. Organised child-care is available for children from the age of 18 months, so women have no problems when they decide to go back to work. One-parent families are not discriminated against, but are actively supported by the state.

During the summer months, when it seems life takes place exclusively outdoors, children play out until midnight. School playgrounds, gardens, roads and beaches are their stomping grounds. Icelandic children are brought up to be independent from an early age, and many teenagers work in shops in the afternoons after school. Since Icelanders are keen consumers, it is natural to want to go to work and earn money as soon as possible.

This orientation towards the family is also evident in pricing. Children under 4 years of age pay nothing and the under-12s generally only half-price; this applies both to public transport fares as well as admission charges.

When touring with children, it's a good idea to stay on farms; many keep livestock and have horses; some offer bird-watching excursions or fishing trips. Huts and cabins are ideal, too; de-

In the land of animals and trolls: how did the Vikings live; what are the whales up to? Iceland has answers to all these questions

pending on the type, they offer plenty of space and often have their own kitchen. Many hotels and guest houses have special family rooms with up to six beds.

In the larger villages there are playgrounds at the campsites, and many swimming pools have special attractions for children, such as slides. Open-air museums offer kids plenty of room to make their own discoveries, especially *Skógar* in the South, *Glaumbær* in the North and *Hnjótur* in the West. Not

surprisingly, the saga museums and reconstructed longhouses, too, offer vivid and exciting encounters with the past.

You can undertake whale-watching excursions from many coastal villages; out at sea, you can learn a lot about the various species of this giant marine mammal. The dolphins are particularly curious, swimming up close to the boats. On walks, you're likely to come across free-roaming mother sheep with their lambs.

ÁRBÆJARSAFN (127 D5) (*ⁿ E9*)

At weekends, the open-air museum offers special children's activities, including courses in old agricultural practices. There is also an interesting exhibition of reindeer, mink and Arctic fox. There's also a small fun park with carousels, boats, miniature racetrack, a BMX course and much more. A restaurant rounds off the list of attractions. *15 May–Aug daily 10am–6pm, Sept–14 May daily 10am–5pm | admission 900 ISK, children (5–12*

Do you see a spout? When will he surface? Is that a fin? Waiting anxiously to spot a whale

old toys. *June–Aug daily 10am–5pm, Sept–May daily 1pm-5pm, guided tours daily 1pm | admission 1700 ISK, children free | Kistuhylur 4 | www.arbaejarsafn.is*

BOAT TRIP (127 D4–5) (*ⁿ E9*)

Why not take a boat trip to have look at the thousands of puffins which live on the islands of and Akurey just off the coast near Reykjavík. *Whale Watching Centre | departure from Ægisgarður harbour | 8700 ISK, children (7–15 years): 4350 ISK | tel. 5 19 50 00 | www.elding.is*

FARM ANIMAL GARDEN
(127 D5) (*ⁿ E9*)

This is the place to see Iceland's farm animals, as well as seals, greylag geese, *years) 680 ISK | Engjavegur | www.mu.is*

Right next door is Reykjavík's *Botanical Garden*, a varied park landscape which is home to around 5000 species of plant, organised according to themes.

WHALES OF ICELAND (U B1) (*ⁿ b1*)

Life-size whales are few and far between, but here you'll find species of whale that live off the coast of Iceland in their true size. The info boards (usually in English) are kid-friendly. After a visit to the whale centre, a whale watching tour is even more exciting. *June–Aug daily 10am–6pm, Sept–May daily 10am–5pm | 2900 ISK, children (7–15 years) 1500 ISK, families 5800 ISK | Fiskislóð 23–25 | www.whales oficeland.is*

THE SOUTH

HEIMAEY (128 A6) (*🛱 G12*)
In August, when the fledgling puffins take to the air, many stray into the small town, attracted by the street lights and the noise. The local children round them up in the night and set them free again the following morning.

THE EAST

JÖKULSÁRLON (130 B5) (*🛱 O10*)
On the Jökulsárlón glacier lagoon, you sail around the huge icebergs and can even suck on a piece of ice. When do you get the chance to ride or even swim with an amphibian boat? A very unique experience that you definitely need to book in advance during the main season. *Tel. 4 78 21 22 | www.icelagoon.is*

THE NORTH

HVAMMSTANGI (121 F5) (*🛱 G–F 4–5*)
Around 35 km/22 miles to the north of Hvammstangi on the west coast of the Vatnsnes Peninsula you are almost sure to be able to spot a few seals: their favourite places to sun themselves and have a rest are near Illugastaðir and Hindisvík. You can find out all about these animals at the INSIDERTIP *Icelandic Seal Center: June–Aug daily 9am–7pm | admission 1100 ISK, children (12–16 years): 750 ISK | Strandgata 1 | Hvammstangi | www.selasetur.is*

INSIDERTIP **JÓLAGARÐURINN** (123 E3) (*🛱 L4*)
This shop for Christmas fans lies 5 km/3 miles south of Akureyri. You can buy Icelandic Christmas decorations and other seasonal items – and there's a café. *June–Aug daily 10am–9pm, Sept–Dec 2pm–9pm, Jan–May 2pm–6pm*

SAFNAHÚSIÐ (HÚSAVÍK MUSEUM) (123 F1) (*🛱 M3*)
Much acclaimed for its natural-history display featuring a stuffed polar bear shot in 1969 on the island of Grimsey, having drifted there on an ice floe from Greenland. *June–15 Sept daily 10am–6pm, 16 Sept–May Mon–Fri 9am–4pm | admission 1200 ISK, children under 16 free | Stórigarður 17 | www.husmus.is*

THE HIGHLANDS

Have you any idea why some blocks of lava look like human figures? It's because they were originally trolls which were turned to stone after failing to return to their caves before the sun came up! You can learn lots more about trolls in the picture book "Icelandic Trolls" by Brian Pilkington, an Icelandic-British illustrator. The book also contains a map identifying the locations of the biggest and most striking trolls in Iceland. In the Highlands in particular, your children can meet many of these charming fellows! Incidentally, trolls are the cause of volcanic eruptions – when they are doing their cooking!

LANGJÖKULL (128 A–B 1–2) (*🛱 G–H 7–8*)
A ride in a dog-sled across the glacier is fun for everyone. The powerful Greenlandic huskies, the name of the breed used, just love racing across the ice. After the ride, you can even say thank you by giving them a friendly pat. If you book a whole day, you'll have the opportunity to learn how to steer a sled and try it out for yourself. In the evening, you get to feed the dogs, too. *Dogsledding Iceland | from 1.5 hrs | 24,900 ISK per person, children under 12 pay half price | tel. 8 63 67 33 | www.dogsledding.is*

FESTIVALS & EVENTS

The Icelanders like to party – where possible, outside – with of course the obligatory masses of hearty food and fortifying drinks. The religious holidays are mostly celebrated within the family, with Christmas playing a special role. The 13 Father Christmases, or "Yule Lads", – a really weird bunch – start to arrive on 12 December, bringing the children a small present every day. The first is the "Sheep-Cote Clod", who leaves again on Christmas Day, and the last one is the "Candle Stealer", arriving on Christmas Eve and returning to the mountains on 6 January, the 13th day of the Christmas period. What's more, it's traditional to dress up in something really smart on Christmas Eve – and it has to be something new, otherwise the Yule Cat will get you!

FESTIVALS & EVENTS

FEBRUARY

Carnival in Iceland goes through the stomach: On Monday *(bolludagur)* it's cream-filled buns and on Shrove Tuesday *(sprengidagur)*, mountains of lamb and peas. On Ash Wednesday *(öskudagur)*, children in fancy dress collect sweets and money.

APRIL

The third Thursday is the *first day of summer* and street party time, whatever the weather – and snow is not uncommon in April!

MAY

The annual ★ *Reykjavík Arts Festival* showcases international and national artists from all genres. In recent years, other Icelandic places have also taken part. *en/listahatid.is/about*

JUNE

To celebrate *Sailors' Day* on the first weekend of June, cultural and sporting events and markets take place in fishing villages all over the island.

The high point is ★ *Independence Day* on 17 June. The official commemoration is on Austurvöllur square in the capital, where the President lays a wreath at the Jón Sigurðsson monument. The *fjalla konan,* the "Lady of the Mountains", sings the praises of the country's beautiful landscape. The unofficial part is a huge street party with bands and stalls.

End of the month: four-day *jazz festival* in Egilsstaðir with musicians from all over Scandinavia. *www.jea.is*

A profusion of parties: silly Santas, sheep-sorting and summer in April

AUGUST

The first weekend is a long one, thanks to the **bank holiday Monda**y, traditionally a day for countryside trips. Heimaey, especially, is overrun with visitors, when Independence Day is celebrated again with rock concerts and firework displays.

In early August, things get a little outrageous when crowds of gays and lesbians fill the streets for their **Gay Pride** parade. On the third weekend, get your trainers on for **Reykjavík Marathon** (www.mara thon.is), followed by INSIDERTIP **Culture Night** with a raft of concerts, readings and exhibitions – all free of charge – and culminating in a firework display.

SEPTEMBER

Farmers on horseback set out to round up their herds of sheep in the Highlands. Back in the villages, they are driven into large pens *(réttur)* and then sorted. The end of this tiring and difficult task is celebrated with music, dancing and food.

This ⭐ **rounding-up ritual** ritual attracts many foreign visitors who may also join in the ride.

OCTOBER

The annual **Film Festival** in Reykjavík features international and Icelandic pictures. The **Iceland Airwaves Festival,** as an alternative festival, presents mostly Icelandic musicians and bands.

NATIONAL HOLIDAYS

1 Jan	**New Year**
Maundy Thursday, Good Friday	
Easter Monday	
3rd Thu in April	**first day of summer**
1 May	**Labour Day**
Ascension, Whit Monday	
17 June	**Independence Day**
1st Mon in Aug	**Bank Holiday**
24–26 Dec	**Christmas**
31 Dec	**New Year's Eve**

LINKS, BLOGS, APPS & MORE

www.samferda.is Free car-pooling service, ideal if you want to get from A to B and don't want to take the conventional hitch-hiking option. A contribution to petrol costs is customary

www.eymundsson.is If you can't make it in person to Iceland's biggest and oldest bookstore, visit their website which has a special visitors section in English. Good source of books on Iceland, CDs and DVDs, too, and the place to order your maps in advance

www.grapevine.is Look no further than the aptly named Grapevine for details of what's happening in Reykjavík and indeed the whole island. Background articles, arts reviews, etc.

www.travelnet.is Bags of information on accommodation, car hire, tour operators and even ideas for where to eat out in Iceland, including useful links

www.icelandreview.com „A window on Icelandic society", to quote its deputy editor, the Iceland Review (also in printed form) has news, reviews, features and events listings

www.icelandmusic.is Icelandic music has become pretty popular; this website will keep you up-to-date about the latests trends and bands

www.iheartreykjavik.net Auður writes an informative blog about Reykjavík and Iceland; her company offers walking tours of Reykjavík

expertvagabond.com/ring-road-trip-iceland Good summary of a trip on the Ring Road with stunning pictures of things you can see on the trip: waterfalls, an airplane wreck, volcanos, icebergs, northern lights...

unlockingkiki.com Blog by an American who ended up in Iceland

Regardless of whether you are still researching your trip or already in Iceland: these addresses will provide you with more information, videos and networks to make your holiday even more enjoyable

icelandeyes.blogspot.de Award-winning blog by a keen photographer. It's no surprise that her pictures – and the ones supplied by guest photographers – are a brilliant advertisement for a trip to Iceland. Scroll down the left for some links to breathtakingly beautiful videos, too

www.inspiredbyiceland.com/ What do I love about Iceland? Follow this shortcut to understand what makes the island so fascinating. There are videos and music clips – some of which are also available on YouTube – and two webcams, one showing bathers at the Blue Lagoon and the other watching the birds on the Tjörnin lake in the middle of Reykjavík

VIDEOS & MUSIC

www.youtube.com/user/britishpathe/search?query=iceland Old films showing everyday life in Reykjavík in the 1930s, from the fishing industry to the occupation during World War II

www.youtube.com/watch?v=RIQqVqQs9Xs Beautiful time-lapse video of the breathtaking Icelandic landscape – ice caves, northern lights, waterfalls and the se

Reykjavík Walking Tours and Map Diverse sights in Reykjavík, along with maps of themed city tours on subjects such as "Museums", "Shopping" or "Nightlife"

APPS

Locatify Iceland Several tours for you to download and undertake under your own steam, such as the "Golden Circle", "Vikings in West Iceland" or a trip to the realm of the "hidden people"

SOS 112 This app is very important for hikers who plan to take several day treks far from the lodges. By pressing a button, you send your coordinates, making a search easier in an emergency

Locals recommend Reykjavík What do the people who live in Reykjavík recommend? This app offers descriptions of restaurants, bars, and shopping options, plus some hotel recommendations

Craving Food & Dining / Appy Hour Happy Hours These apps from the free magazine *Grapevine* cover more than just culinary events.

TRAVEL TIPS

ACCOMMODATION

With the exception of Radisson SAS or Hilton you will only find Icelandic hotel chains. There are, for example, nine Icelandair hotels offering luxury facilities (*www.icehotels.is*). They are followed by the twelve Foss hotels, often in very charming locations but unfortunately often totally overpriced (*www.fosshotel. is*). The twelve Edda hotels offer summertime accommodation in boarding schools and colleges; many have a swimming pool, restaurant and their own bar, and the rooms have a shower and WC. A number of these hotels offer sleeping bag accommodation as an alternative (*www.hoteledda.is*).

Icelandic Farm Holidays is an association of farms which provide not only accommodation but also a range of activities, such as riding, fishing, hunting, swimming and the chance to participate in the annual rounding-up of sheep from the summer pastures. Brochure and information: *Icelandic Farm Holidays (Reykjavík | Siðumúla 13 | tel. 5 70 27 00 | www.farm holidays.is)*. Some of the farms have cottages for rent.

A number of tour operators rent out private summer cottages or holiday apartments, but these often have to be booked for a minimum of one week, e.g. at *katla-travel.is.* Viator is another company on the island (*www.viator.is*).

Despite the wide range of choices, some tourists are disappointed because many hotels and private accommodation providers also offer very small rooms that seem to be overpriced.

INSIDER TIP ▶ Affordable four-star stays are to be had if you book via the Internet, ideally outside the summer season. You might pick up an offer with up to 50 per cent discount on the regular price.

RESPONSIBLE TRAVEL

It doesn't take a lot to be environmentally friendly whilst travelling. Don't just think about your carbon footprint whilst flying to and from your holiday destination but also about how you can protect nature and culture abroad. As a tourist it is especially important to respect nature, look out for local products, cycle instead of driving, save water and much more. If you would like to find out more about eco-tourism please visit: *www.ecotourism.org*

ARRIVAL

✈ Since Iceland has become such an immensely popular travel destination, the number of flights to the island has consequently risen. *Icelandair*, the oldest national carrier, flies from London. The price system is rather complicated, but it is possible to book reasonably priced flights by doing so early and flying outside the high season in summer. Be sure to compare offers from other airlines (*www.icelandair.is*). The second Icelandic airline is *WOW Air* which also departs from London as well as Edinburgh, Bristol, Cork and Dublin. Flights are generally cheaper (*www. wowair.com*). Budget carrier Easyjet offers connections from London, Bristol, Edinburgh, Manchester and Belfast

From arrival to weather

Your holiday from start to finish: the most important addresses and information for your trip to Iceland

(www.easyjet.com). KLM flies from New York direct to Reykjavík, the trip taking around 6 hours *(www.klm.com)*. Look on the website of Keflavík Airport for an up-to-date list of other carriers currently serving Reykjavík; in recent years these have been known to change frequently *(www.kefairport.is)*.

Buses run from Keflavík to the BSÍ bus station in Reykjavík (45 minutes), where you can transfer to other bus lines. ● Buying your return journey online is considerably cheaper than two single tickets. *www.flybus.is*

You can take the "Norröna" ferry, operated by *Smyril Line*, to travel from Hirtshals (Denmark) to Seyðisfjörður. Mid-June to Mid-August: Depart Hirtshals Sat 3:30pm, arrive in Seyðisfjörður on Thu at 9:30am with a four-day stay on the Faroe Islands; Depart Seyðisfjörður Thu 11:30am, arrive in Hirtshals Sat 12:30pm. Late March to Mid-June and Late August to October, depart Hirtshals Sat 3pm, arrive in Seyðisfjörður Tue 9am. The ferry runs as a cargo ship in winter, but still takes on passengers. Costs for 2 people (with their private car) and sleeping berths: from 599 euros (if booked early on-line), otherwise from 880 euros in peak season and 501 euros in the off-season. *www.smyril-line.com*

BANKS & CURRENCY

Opening times: Mon–Fri 9.15am–4pm. You can withdraw cash using your credit card from the ATMs. Mastercard and Visa are accepted nationwide.

The Icelandic currency is the *króna* (ISK). There are coins to the value of 1, 5, 10, 50 and 100 ISK as well as banknotes valued at 500, 1000, 2000, 5000 and 10,000 ISK.

CAMPING

There are 170 campsites with various types of facilities, most of which are only open in the summer. Standards differ greatly, depending on the location: town/village or Highlands. On average you can expect to pay around 2000 ISK per person per night plus the tent. With the INSIDER TIP ▶ *Camping Card* for around

CURRENCY CONVERTER

£	ISK	ISK	£
1	158	2	0.01
3	474	10	0.06
5	789	25	0.16
13	2052	80	0.51
40	6315	150	0.95
75	11,841	500	3.17
120	18,945	1200	7.60
250	39,500	10,000	63.34
500	79,000	50,000	317

$	ISK	ISK	$
1	124	2	0.02
3	373	10	0.08
5	622	25	0.20
13	1618	80	0.64
40	4979	150	1.20
75	9300	500	4.02
120	15,000	1200	9.64
250	31,000	10,000	80.33
500	62,000	50,000	402

For current exchange rates see www.xe.com

20,700 ISK, you can pitch your tent on 41 sites. It is valid for two adults and up to four children (under 16 years of age). You can have the card sent to your home address before embarking on your holiday. *www.campingcard.is*

There are other camping sites in many of the smaller places, most of them are situated directly next to the swimming pool *(www.nat.is/camping-in-iceland)*. Wild camping in a tent or camper van is not permitted.

CAR HIRE

Almost all larger places have a car-hire firm. It always pays to compare prices offered by the various companies; the smallest models cost around 9700 ISK per day in the summer. Hire cars are relatively new and suited to Icelandic driving conditions. Drivers must be at least 20 years of age – for off-road vehicles, 23 – and have had a driving licence for at least one year. If you take your hire car into the Highlands or on rough, off-road trails, you will be fined accordingly. All costs arising from ensuing damage will be borne by the person hiring the vehicle.

CLIMATE, WHEN TO GO

The most popular time to travel to Iceland is from June to August, with the highest average temperatures hitting 13°C/55°F, the likelihood of rain at its lowest and the days are longest. An ideal holiday time is September, the only true autumnal month. At this time, when Iceland is cloaked in myriad golden hues, your chances of having the country – almost – to yourself are relatively good. In addition, the tradition of driving the sheep down into the valleys is celebrated in numerous festivals. Another good time to go is May, when the days are long and the first buds and blossoms are appearing. It's also the time for the *Reykjavík Art Festival*, and outdoor life gets under way in earnest. In the winter, it can get very cold on account of the wind; on the other hand, this is the best time for a sighting of the Northern Lights. Iceland is notorious for its changeable weather, so don't forget to pack your waterproofs and a warm jumper.

CONSULATES & EMBASSIES

UK EMBASSY
101 Reykjavík | Laufásvegur 31 | tel. 5 50 51 00 | info@britishembassy.is | ukiniceland.fco.gov.uk
US EMBASSY
101 Reykjavík | Laufásvegur 21 | tel. 5 95 22 00 | iceland.usembassy.gov

CUSTOMS

Adults may bring goods into Iceland duty- and tax-free as follows (in the case of alcohol, the minimum age is 20): 1 l alcohol up to 47 per cent, either 1 l of wine up to 21 per cent and 6 l of beer or 12 l beer, 200 cigarettes or 250 g of other tobacco products, foodstuffs up to 3 kg. It is prohibited to bring in animals, narcotics, fresh meat, fresh dairy products and eggs. Information under *www.tollur.is*

You are not permitted to take the following out of Iceland: protected plants, egg shells, birds' eggs, nests, birds, pieces of stone broken out of caves or any other protected monuments. Historical or archaeological artefacts may also not be exported.

DRIVING

The statutory speed limit in built-up areas is 50 km/h (31 mph), on overland roads with gravel surface 80 km/h (50 mph) and 90 km/h (56 mph) on asphalt. The loose gravel offers vehicles little grip, and you must be careful when swerving to avoid oncoming traffic on the often narrow roads.

Warning signs with the word "blindhæð" indicate blind rises crossing hills. Animals, such as free-roaming sheep, always have right of way in Iceland. It is compulsory to drive with dipped headlights, even during the day. All persons travelling in the vehicle must wear a seatbelt. The blood-alcohol limit is 0 per cent.

For driving in the Highlands, you'll need an off-road vehicle. In the summer, the Icelandic Road Administration, in collaboration with the Iceland Nature Conservation Association, issues a map which is updated every week showing which routes across the Highlands are open to traffic. If you drive on such a trail before it has been officially declared open, you can be fined; the police regularly monitor traffic, also from the air. It is also strictly prohibited to drive outside the marked trails. Information: *www.vegagerdin.is*

Apart from in the Highlands, there is a fairly dense network of petrol stations. In Reykjavík and the larger towns, they are generally open until midnight. Here, you can often fill up and pay using 500- or 1000-ISK notes or credit cards at self-service machines. Unleaded petrol (95 octane and 98 octane) as well as diesel *(dísel)* are available.

ment *(slysadeild)* at a hospital *(sjúkrahús)* or contact a doctor *(læknir)* directly. Medical bills must be paid in cash. Find out from your medical insurance company before your travel which costs will be covered, and take out separate travel health insurance for your trip, if necessary.

BUDGETING

Bus ride	3.90 $ / 3.10 £
	for a ticket on Reykjavík's buses
Souvenir	from 168 $ / 133 £
	for an Icelandic pullover
Beer	from 6.75 $ / 5.30 £
	for 0.5 l in a bar
Coffee	from 3.10 $ / 2 £
	for two cups
Snack	2.25 $ / 1.75 £
	for a Skyr with fruit
Swimming pool	9 $ / 7 £
	admission charge in Reykjavík

Pharmacies *(apótek)* are recognisable by the sign with a cross and the words "Lyf og heilsa". They are open during normal business hours, and there is usually one on duty around the clock in Reykjavík. If you are dependent on regular medication, be sure to take a sufficient stock with you, in case it is not possible to obtain precisely the same products in Iceland.

EMERGENCY SERVICES

Nationwide emergency telephone number: 112

HEALTH

In the event of serious illness or an accident, you should contact the A&E depart-

HOSTELS

The 34 youth hostels are available to everyone and there are no age restrictions. Information, including brochures with descriptions, is available from the youth hostel association *Bandalag Íslenskra Farfugla (Reykjavík | Borgartún 6 | tel. 575 67 00 | www.hostel.is)*.

IMMIGRATION

For travellers from Schengen countries, there is no passport control; others will of course be checked as normal. If you are bringing your own vehicle into Iceland, you must carry your passport, vehicle registration documents, proof of valid insurance cover ("green card") and your driving licence. Drivers from the UK, US, Canada, Australia, New Zealand and most European countries can use their standard licence; others should check whether they need an international licence. Items of horseriding clothing and equipment which have been used outside Iceland first have to be disinfected by a vet and you will need to present an official certificate on arrival. Otherwise, the items will be disinfected for you at a cost on arrival.

INFORMATION

PRE-TRAVEL
Comprehensive information on Iceland, brochures for downloading: *Icelandic Tourist Office | www.visiticeland.com*

Icelandic Tourist Board in the USA | c/o The Scandinavian Tourist Board | 655 Third Avenue | New York, NY 10017 | tel. 212 8 85 97 00 | www.visiticeland.com

IN ICELAND
Ferðamálaráð Íslands | Geirsgata 9 | 101 Reykjavík | Tel. 5 35 55 00 | www.visitice land.com
– *www.iceland.is:* Iceland's official site, on which it showcases nature, culture and the economy. The comprehensive list of links is an excellent source of information.

WEATHER IN REYKJAVÍK

	Jan	Feb	March	April	May	June	July	Aug	Sept	Oct	Nov	Dec
Daytime temperatures in °C/°F	2/36	3/37	5/41	6/43	10/50	13/55	15/59	14/57	12/54	8/46	5/41	4/40
Nighttime temperatures in °C/°F	–3/27	–3/27	–1/30	1/34	4/40	7/45	9/48	8/46	6/43	3/37	0/32	–2/29
☀ Sunshine hours/day	1	2	4	5	7	5	7	6	4	3	2	1
☂ Precipitation days/month	14	12	12	12	10	10	10	12	13	14	14	15
≈ Water temperature in °C/°F	4	4	4	5	7	9	11	11	10	7	6	5

☀ Sunshine hours/day ☂ Precipitation days/month ≈ Water temperature in °C/°F

INTERNET & WIFI

Icelanders are among the world's keenest Internet users, so it's no surprise to find hotspots in the large hotels – often in the entrance hall – and Internet access in rooms. Many cafés and restaurants offer WiFi, too.

MEDIA

The BBC World Service broadcasts 24 hours a day on 90.9 FM. International newspapers can be bought at larger bookshops in Reykjavík, usually one day after publication. "Grapevine" is a free English-language newspaper available at many outlets.

OPENING HOURS

Shops are open as follows: Mon–Fri 9am–6pm, Sat 9am–4pm. Some supermarkets are open 24 hours, 7 days a week. The *Kringlan* shopping centre in Reykjavík and *Smáralind* in Kópavogur have extended opening on Thursdays and open on Sundays (except in summer). Kiosks *(sjópa)* are usually open for business until 11.30pm, selling drinks and a small range of foods. Restaurants and also the tourist information offices are generally open every day.

PHONE & MOBILE PHONE

Telephone calls to Iceland: dial 00354, then the 7-digit number. Calling from Iceland: UK 0044, USA 001; then the area code without the 0.

POST

There are post offices *(póstur)* in all towns and larger villages. Opening times: Mon–Fri 9am–6pm. Air-mail letters and post-cards up to 20 g within Europe cost from 165 ISK. *www.postur.is*

PRICES & TIPPING

Prices tend to be a good deal higher than the rest of Europe. Alcoholic beverages are particularly expensive. *Bónus* shops are the cheapest place to buy groceries. Tips are included in the price at restaurants, and Icelanders don't add extra. Many tourists still give an additional tip, but it is not expected.

PUBLIC TRANSPORT

Iceland has an extensive public bus network, and in the summer months several bus passes are on offer with reduced fares. You can get on and off at any point along the route. Information on tours, timetables, fares and special offers: *Destination Iceland (BSÍ bus station | www.bsi.is)*. Reykjavík has its own city bus network.

Air Iceland and Eagle Air fly to various destinations in Iceland and also offer charter flights. The offers listed on the Internet are the cheapest. Information: *www.ernir.is* and *www.airiceland.is*

SAFETY

To avoid emergencies on walks, in the mountains, on glaciers or in the highlands, we recommend reading the safety recommendations at *safetravel.is*. This website provides extensive information on road blocks, landslides, closed bridges, dangerous river fording etc.

TIME

Iceland uses Greenwich Mean Time (GMT) all year round.

ROAD ATLAS

The green line indicates the Discovery Tour "Iceland at a glance"
The blue line indicates the other Discovery Tours

All tours are also marked on the pull-out map

Photo: Bog cotton meadow in Landmannalaugar

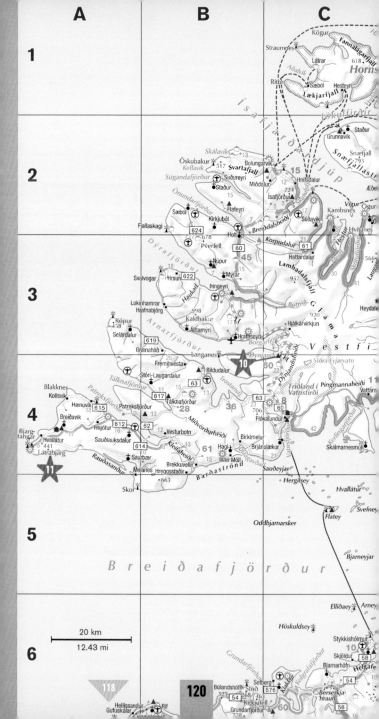

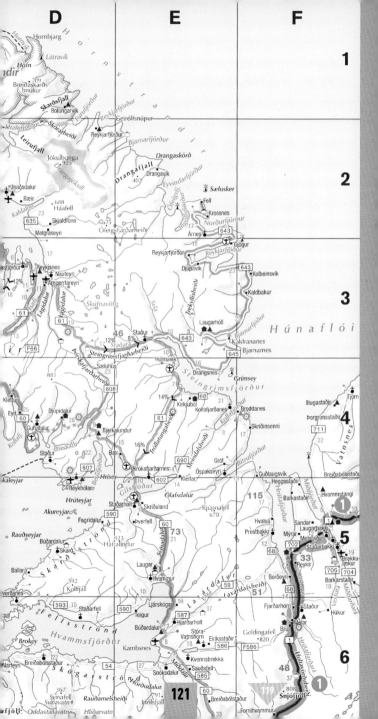

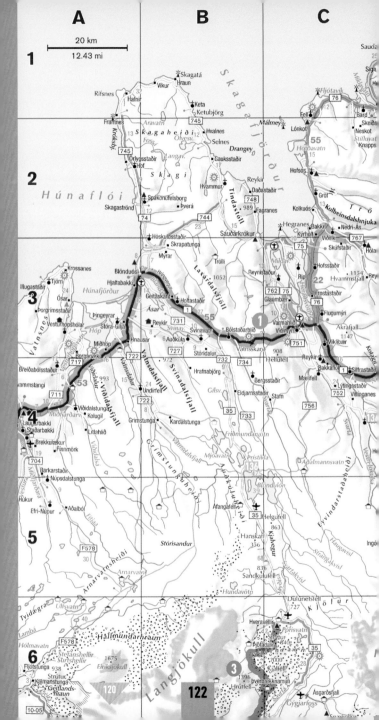

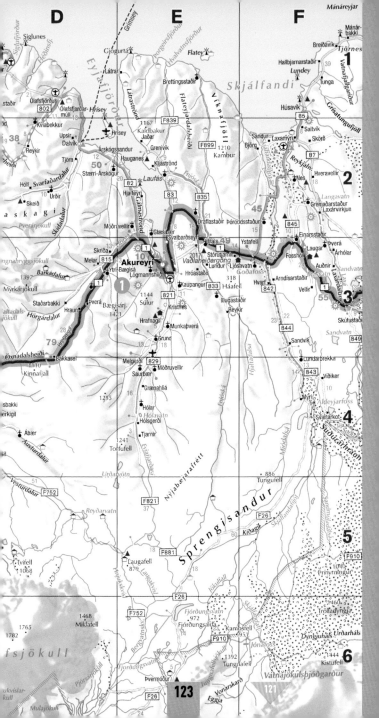

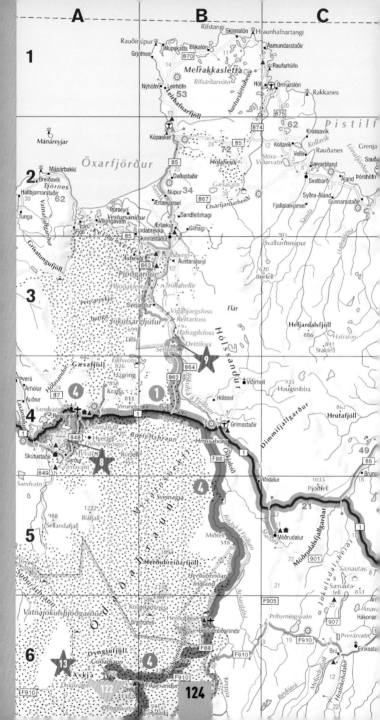

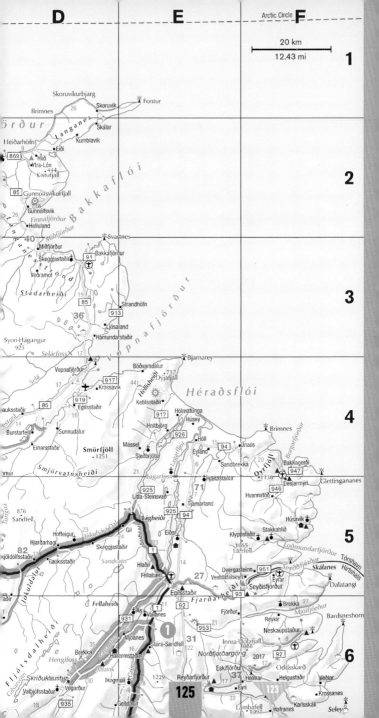

Arctic Circle

20 km
12.43 mi

1

2

3

4

5

6

Skoruvíkurbjarg
Brimnes
·jörður Langanes
Skoruvík
Fontur
Skálar
Heiðarhöfn
869
Eiði
Ytra-Lón ·444
Kistufjall
85 Gunnólfsvíkurfjall
Gunnólfsvík
·118
Helluland
Finnafjörður
40 Miðfjörður
Svartnes
Miðfjörður
91 Bakkafjörður
Skeggjastaðir
Veðramót
Staðarheiði
19
85
Strandhöfn
913
Ljósaland
Syðri-Hágangur Hámundarstaðir
·925
Selárfoss 17
Vopnafjörður
Böðvarsdalur
Bjarnarey
Hellisheiði 717
Dyrfjall
917 44
Krossavík
Héraðsflói
919 Egilsstaðir
Ketilsstaðir
Hólmatunga
Húsey
85
Hnitbjörg
Brimnes
Burstarfell
926
Höll
Unaós
94
Smörfjöll Mássel
Eyland
·1251 Sléðbrjótur
Sandbrekka 20 Bakkagerði
Smjörvatnsheiði
Hjaltastaðir
Dyrfjöll ·1136 947
946 Desjarmýri
Glettinganes
Litla-Steinsvað
925
Hvannstóð
·876 Sandfell
Lagheiði
Húsavík
Hofteigur Gil
925 Tjarnarland
Stakkahlíð
Hjarðarhagi Skeggjastaðir
94 Eiðar
Klyppstaðir
82 Gauksstaðir
1 ·1055 Eldfell
jöldólfsstaðir
Hlaðir
Dvergasteinn 951 Skálanes
Torshavn
Fellabær
27 Vestdalseyri Eyrar Hirtshals
Egilsstaðir Seyðisfjörður Dalatangi
Fellaheiði Fjarðarheiði 93
Ás 92 Fjörður Brekka
931 Vallanes Reykir Bardsneshorn
Mjóanes 953 Neskaupstaður
Brekka Innra-Hólafjall ·1088
Hallormsstaður Stóra-Sandfell 31 Norðfjarðargöng 92
Þingmúli ·1229 22 2017
Eskifjörður Oddsskarð
Atlavík 37 123 Helgustaðir
Skriðuklaustur Vegarður Reyðarfjörður Hólmar Veðlar
Valþjófsstaður Geitdalur Eyri Krossanes
935 1229 Lambafell Hafranes Karlsskáli Seley

125

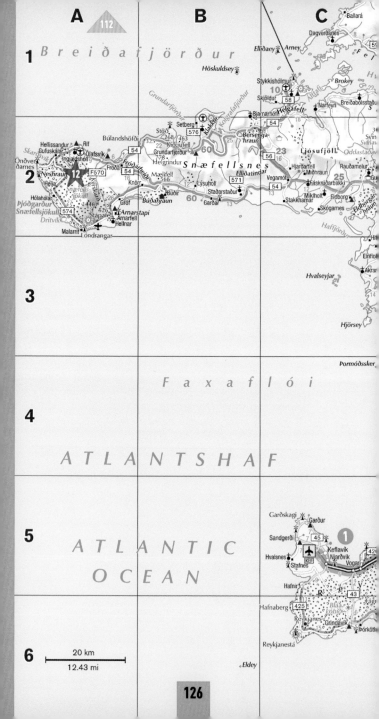

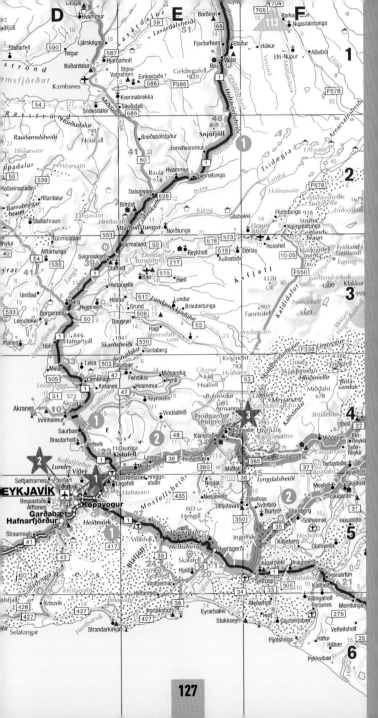

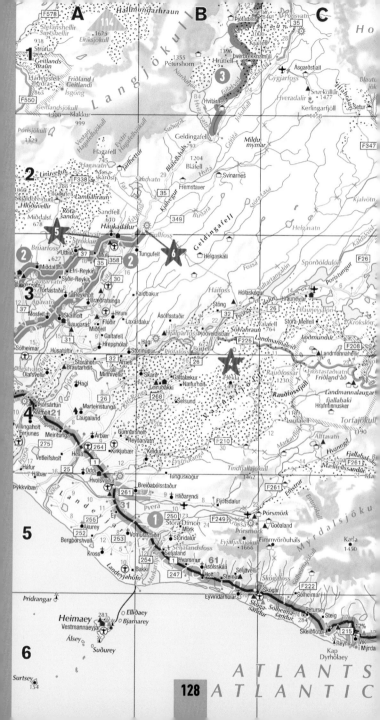

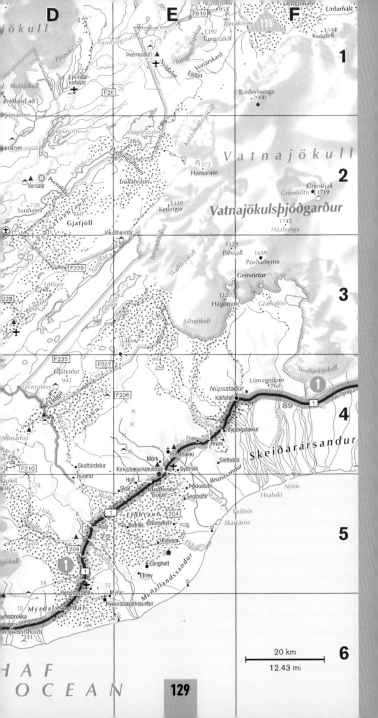

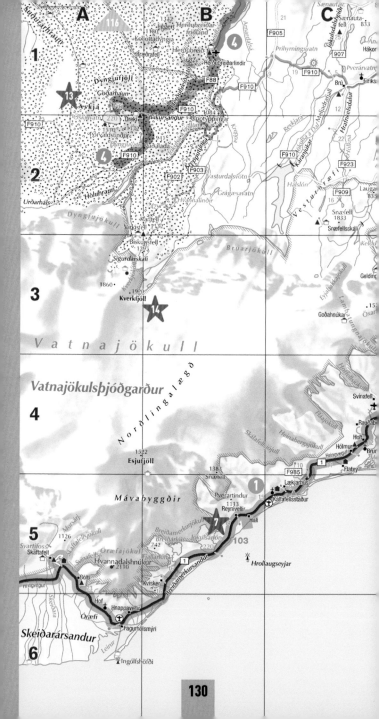

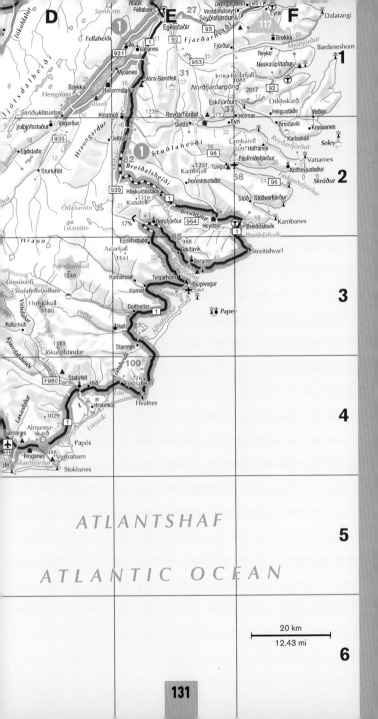

KEY TO ROAD ATLAS

German		English
Durchgangsstraße - Wichtige Hauptstraße	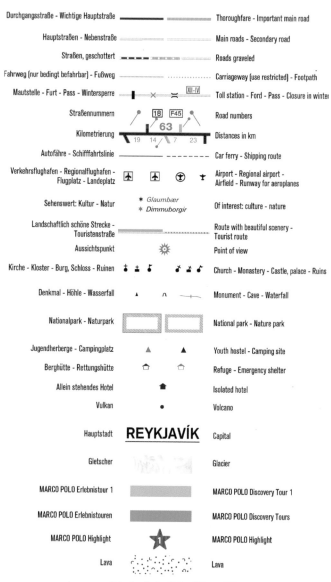	Thoroughfare - Important main road
Hauptstraßen - Nebenstraße		Main roads - Secondary road
Straßen, geschottert		Roads graveled
Fahrweg (nur bedingt befahrbar) - Fußweg		Carriageway (use restricted) - Footpath
Mautstelle - Furt - Pass - Wintersperre		Toll station - Ford - Pass - Closure in winter
Straßennummern		Road numbers
Kilometrierung		Distances in km
Autofähre - Schifffahrtslinie		Car ferry - Shipping route
Verkehrsflughafen - Regionalflughafen - Flugplatz - Landeplatz		Airport - Regional airport - Airfield - Runway for aeroplanes
Sehenswert: Kultur - Natur		Of interest: culture - nature
Landschaftlich schöne Strecke - Touristenstraße		Route with beautiful scenery - Tourist route
Aussichtspunkt		Point of view
Kirche - Kloster - Burg, Schloss - Ruinen		Church - Monastery - Castle, palace - Ruins
Denkmal - Höhle - Wasserfall		Monument - Cave - Waterfall
Nationalpark - Naturpark		National park - Nature park
Jugendherberge - Campingplatz		Youth hostel - Camping site
Berghütte - Rettungshütte		Refuge - Emergency shelter
Allein stehendes Hotel		Isolated hotel
Vulkan		Volcano
Hauptstadt		Capital
Gletscher		Glacier
MARCO POLO Erlebnistour 1		MARCO POLO Discovery Tour 1
MARCO POLO Erlebnistouren		MARCO POLO Discovery Tours
MARCO POLO Highlight		MARCO POLO Highlight
Lava		Lava

Lava area © Icelandic Institute of Natural History

MARCO POLO TRAVEL GUIDES

Algarve
Amsterdam
Andalucia
Athens
Australia
Austria
Bali & Lombok
Bangkok
Barcelona
Berlin
Brazil
Bruges
Brussels
Budapest
Bulgaria
California
Cambodia
Canada East
Canada West / Rockies & Vancouver
Cape Town & Garden Route
Cape Verde
Channel Islands
Chicago & The Lakes
China
Cologne
Copenhagen
Corfu
Costa Blanca & Valencia
Costa Brava
Costa del Sol & Granada
Costa Rica
Crete
Cuba
Cyprus (North and South)
Devon & Cornwall
Dresden
Dubai

Dublin
Dubrovnik & Dalmatian Coast
Edinburgh
Egypt
Egypt Red Sea Resorts
Finland
Florence
Florida
French Atlantic Coast
French Riviera (Nice, Cannes & Monaco)
Fuerteventura
Gran Canaria
Greece
Hamburg
Hong Kong & Macau
Ibiza
Iceland
India
India South
Ireland
Israel
Istanbul
Italy
Japan
Jordan
Kos
Krakow
Lake District
Lake Garda
Lanzarote
Las Vegas
Lisbon
London
Los Angeles
Madeira & Porto Santo
Madrid
Maldives
Mallorca
Malta & Gozo
Mauritius

Menorca
Milan
Montenegro
Morocco
Munich
Naples & Amalfi Coast
New York
New Zealand
Norway
Oslo
Oxford
Paris
Peru & Bolivia
Phuket
Portugal
Prague
Rhodes
Rome
Salzburg
San Francisco
Santorini
Sardinia
Scotland
Seychelles
Shanghai
Sicily
Singapore
South Africa
Sri Lanka
Stockholm
Switzerland
Tenerife
Thailand
Tokyo
Turkey
Turkey South Coast
Tuscany
United Arab Emirates
USA Southwest (Las Vegas, Colorado, New Mexico, Arizona & Utah)
Venice
Vienna
Vietnam
Zakynthos & Ithaca, Kefalonia, Lefkas

Travel with Insider Tips

INDEX

This index lists all places, sights and destinations mentioned in the guide. Page numbers in bold type refer to the main entry.

WRITE TO US

e-mail: info@marcopologuides.co.uk

Did you have a great holiday?
Is there something on your mind?
Whatever it is, let us know!
Whether you want to praise, alert us
to errors or give us a personal tip –
MARCO POLO would be pleased to
hear from you.
We do everything we can to provide the
very latest information for your trip.

Nevertheless, despite all of our authors'
thorough research, errors can creep in.
MARCO POLO does not accept any
liability for this. Please contact us by
e-mail or post.

MARCO POLO Travel Publishing Ltd
Pinewood, Chineham Business Park
Crockford Lane, Chineham
Basingstoke, Hampshire RG24 8AL
United Kingdom

PICTURE CREDITS
Cover Photograph: Godafoss waterfall (Look/age fotostock)
Photos: Café Oliver: Halldór Kolbeins (18 top); Getty Images: DaniloAndjus (3), F. Cui-Paoluzzo (109), F. Gentile (12/13, 111), I. Gethings (44/45), A. Stricher (46), T. E. White (66); Getty Images/Corbis Documentary/Arctic-Images (7); Heydalur: Anna Ruesch (19 top); huber-images: C. Dörr (122/123), L. Grandadam (48), M. Rellini (20/21, 74, 80), M. Robertz (53); O. Krüger (29); Laif: C. Boisvieux (91), P. Frilet (30), M. Galli (flap left, 5, 32/33, 37), G. Hänel (72), Henseler (28 right), B. Jonkmanns (106), T. Linkel (30/31, 64, 96); Laif/hemis.fr: Boisberranger (6), M. Cavalier (77), Rieger (10); Laif/Le Figaro Magazine: Gladieu (9); Laif/Redux/Herd In Iceland: L. Blatt (31); Laif/Redux/VWPics: M. Bilbao (99); Laif/robertharding: P. Dieudonne (70/71); Look: Eisele-Hein (103), J. Greune (38), R. Mirau (17); Look/age fotostock (1, 69, 108); Look/Aurora Photos (11); Look/SagaPhoto (14, 42/43); mauritius images: C. Lux (59); mauritius images/age: L. Castañeda (4 top, 86/87), R. T. Sigurdsson (51, 62/63), M. Zwick (8); mauritius images/Alamy: K. Cavanagh (flap right, 110 top), J. Eales (18 centre), G. F. Steinsson (28 left); mauritius images/Cultura: Henn Photography (26/27, 100/101), G. Karbus Photography (4 bottom, 22); mauritius images/imagebroker: D. Weyand (2); mauritius images/Prisma: M. Galli (41); mauritius images/United Archives (34); Olvisholt Brugghus: Ófeigur Örn Ófeigsson (19 bottom); picture-alliance/AA: T. Akmen (108/109); picture-alliance/AP Photo: C. Paris (25); Nada Quenzel (18 bottom); vario images/Cultura: E. T. Magnusson (104/105), Y. Timashov (78/79); vario images/imagebroker: O. Krüger (84, 110 bottom), M. Peuckert (83), F. C. Robiller (61), E. Schmidbauer (54/55), F. Scholz (56)

3ⁿᵈ Edition – fully revised and updated 2020
Worldwide Distribution: Marco Polo Travel Publishing Ltd, Pinewood, Chineham Business Park, Crockford Lane, Basingstoke, Hampshire RG24 8AL, United Kingdom. Email: sales@marcopolouk.com
© MAIRDUMONT GmbH & Co. KG, Ostfildern
Chief editor: Stefanie Penck; Author: Sabine Barth, Editor: Arnd M. Schuppius
Programme supervision: Stephan Dürr, Lucas Forst-Gill, Susanne Heimburger, Nikolai Michaelis, Martin Silbermann, Kristin Wittemann; Picture editors: Gabriele Forst, Anja Schlatterer; What's hot: wunder media, Munich; Cartography road atlas: © MAIRDUMONT, Ostfildern; Cartography pull-out map: © MAIRDUMONT, Ostfildern
Design: milchhof : atelier, Berlin; Front cover, pull-out map cover, page 1: Karl Anders - Büro für Visual Stories, Hamburg; Discovery Tours, p. 2/3: Susan Chaaban, Dipl-Des. (FH)
Translated from German by Jennifer Walcoff Neuheiser, Tübingen, Susan Jones, Tübingen
Prepress: writehouse, Cologne; InterMedia, Ratingen

MIX
Paper from
responsible sources
FSC® C124385

DOS & DON'TS 👆

Respect Iceland's countryside – in every way

DON'T TRAVEL IN HIGH SEASON

Everyone loves the summer, but if you want to experience Iceland at its most natural and don't want to share every location with a busload of other tourists, you shouldn't travel during the high season (mid-June to August). At other times, or even in winter, Iceland can truly live up to its reputation of offering you nature at its finest.

DON'T SHOWER IN SWIMWEAR

In swimming pools, you are explicitly requested to shower – without your bathing costume – before swimming. Icelandic pools are not treated with chlorine, and for this reason, hygiene is a top priority. So just do as the Icelanders do and you won't automatically stick out as being a tourist.

DON'T BE UNDERDRESSED

The Icelanders set great store by looking well-groomed and dress with the appropriate degree of elegance when they go out, say, for a night on the town. For Reykjavík especially, it makes good sense to pack a few suitable items of clothing – after all, you are visiting a European capital. Would you feel comfortable savouring a fine wine by candlelight in an exquisite restaurant wearing a check shirt and hiking trousers? Even some discotheques have their own dress code.

DON'T DISTURB THE BIRDS

Photographing and filming the nests of endangered species, such as eagles, falcons, snowy owls and little auks, is punishable by law. Alternatively, you could buy yourself one of the excellent bird books when you're in Iceland and share the expert's-eye view.

DON'T IGNORE WEATHER WARNINGS

If you are driving or hiking in the Highlands, get yourself some up-to-date information from locals who know the area with regard to weather prospects and the nature of the terrain you'll be encountering. If someone tells you that what you have in mind could be difficult, take them very seriously. The weather is extremely changeable, and a sandstorm in the Highlands can turn out to be really unpleasant. Snow storms can occur until June and again from September onwards; they can impair your vision completely and could force you to remain in one place for several days. Make sure you always have a snow shovel in the car with you.

DON'T LEAVE YOUR SHOES ON

When you enter an Icelandic home, you should usually take off your shoes. Only leave them on if your host tells you to. It's definitely more polite to take them off!